# BROTHER, CAN YOU SPARE A DIME?

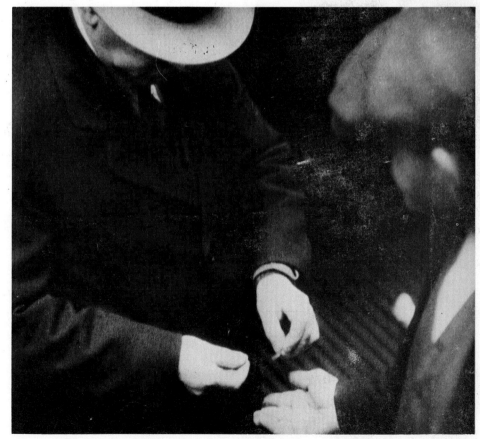

# BROTHER, CAN YOU SPARE A DIME?

America
from the Wall Street Crash
to Pearl Harbor

An Illustrated Documentary
by Susan Winslow
assisted by Wendy Holmes

PADDINGTON
PRESS LTD

THE TWO CONTINENTS
PUBLISHING GROUP

To my mother and father

**Acknowledgments**
The author would like to
acknowledge and thank the
following: the producer, Sandy
Lieberson and director, Philippe
Mora, of the film *Brother, Can You
Spare a Dime?* for the opportunity
and inspiration to do this book;
Janet Hayman, Marie Faller,
Marjorie Winslow and Kevin
Brown for additional research;
Richard Winslow, Dick Speidel,
Michael Brooks, Joe Adamson,
Kate Winslow and Colin Berwick
for their general assistance; and
most particularly, Wendy Holmes,
without whose special contribution
in research and editing, this book
could not have been done.

Page 152 *New Yorker* article from
**The Talk of the Town**. Reprinted
by permission: © 1940, 1968 *The
New Yorker* Magazine
Page 111 **Every Man a King** ©
copyright 1935 Bourne Co., copyright
renewed. Used by permission
For further acknowledgments, see
page 160

A *Webb&Bower* Book
Created by
Webb & Bower Limited,
Exeter, England

Designed by Paul Watkins

Printed in USA
Published by Paddington Press Ltd.,
New York, London

IN THE UNITED STATES
**Paddington Press Ltd**
Two Continents Publishing Group

IN THE UNITED KINGDOM
**Paddington Press Ltd**

IN CANADA
distributed by
**Random House of Canada Ltd**

IN AUSTRALIA & NEW ZEALAND
distributed by
**Angus & Robertson Pty Ltd**

**Library of Congress Cataloging in Publication Data**
Main entry under title:

Brother, can you spare a dime?

Includes index.
1. United States—History—1933-1945.    2. United
States—Economic conditions—1918-1945.    3. United
States—Social conditions—1933-1945.    4. United States
—Social life and customs—1918-1945.    I. Winslow,
Susan, 1951-
E806.B79        973.917        76-3807
ISBN 0-8467-0139-1

# Contents

# Introduction

The 1920's in America were a festival of national naïveté. Perhaps the day hadn't quite yet arrived when there were 'two chickens in every pot and two cars in every garage,' but it was certainly on its way. In the meantime, and perhaps to speed up the process, why not buy a few shares of stock? After all, credit was as good as cash, so what was there to lose? The rich, of course, were getting richer; but it finally seemed that the American middle class was within reach of their rightful piece of the pie. The Great American Dream was coming true at last . . . But in order to be dreaming, one must be asleep.

That sleep was finally and unalterably broken in October, 1929, with the crash of the stock market. Americans woke up to a nightmarish reality: business took a dive and 'security' was suddenly a thing of the past. But no one would have thought so by listening to President Hoover, who declared in December, 1929, that 'any lack of confidence in the economic future of this country . . . is foolish'; or to Secretary of the Treasury Andrew Mellon, who in January, 1930, saw 'nothing in the present situation that is either menacing or warrants pessimism.' As pronouncements of this kind become more frequent and more insistent, conditions steadily deteriorated: people were losing their jobs, homes were repossessed, food supplies began to disappear. Even as late as March, 1931, Henry Ford announced, 'There is plenty of work to do, if people would do it.' But he was wrong: by 1932 there were 15 million Americans unemployed out of a population of about 123 million—and it was not because of any lack of initiative in the labor force.

And this is only the beginning of one of the most dynamic periods in recent American history. It is convenient to call it 'the 1930's,' but it is really a decade of twelve years, with a clear-cut beginning—the Wall Street crash of 1929—and a clear-cut end—the bombing of Pearl Harbor in 1941.

America grew up in these years. In fact, it can almost be said that the changes effected in the 1930's have a more basic and direct relationship to America in the 1970's than do the events of any of the three intervening decades. The Presidency under Roosevelt developed into an office of great centralized power attended by a vast federal bureaucracy; labor fought for and won the right to organize and bargain collectively; and the United States became the leading international power in the Western hemisphere. None of this happened without a struggle. The 1930's were a period of constant political, social, and racial conflict—even conflict with nature. Paradoxically, it was also a time of great optimism and faith. Perhaps this quality was what allowed the conflict to be so intense and ultimately so productive. People had ideals. They fought for their ideals and truly believed they could win. Cynicism had not yet taken over the national character.

It wasn't all hard work, though. Americans could escape into the exploits of their heroes: there was Lindbergh, who was rich and poised and kept breaking records in the air; Dillinger, who robbed from the rich (that he didn't hand over his loot to the poor seemed to matter very little); and Will Rogers, who was just plain folk and kept America laughing at itself. If real-life characters didn't fit the bill, there was Hollywood—the wonderful fantasy world of Shirley Temple, Clark Gable, Charlie Chaplin, Greta Garbo and Busby Berkeley's dancing girls.

And then there was Roosevelt, who above all else was a leader when America needed a leader. He dominated American life as no President has ever done before or has done since.

*Brother, Can You Spare a Dime?* is an outgrowth of the deep excitement I feel for the 1930's. I have come to realize that this period— its cast of characters, their ideas and their deeds—were absolutely crucial to the formation of present-day American values. The impact of these years is felt by all Americans—naturally by those who lived through them, but also by those born many years later.

I have been researching the subject for two and a half years: first doing film research in a newsreel library for the movie of the same name, then photo research, and throughout this time constant reading. I found that the most vivid words I read, and the most truthful, were written in the 30's about the 30's—words that weren't colored with the judgment of time. The speeches, fiction, letters, newspaper reports, diaries, magazine articles and songs all came alive and told so much more than any historical text.

*Brother, Can You Spare a Dime?* is a collection of these writings structured more or less chronologically, and although it is an anthology of sorts, it is organized to be read as a continuous narrative, a history which bares feelings as well as facts. The events and reactions, the politics and human struggles, tell their own story and sometimes contradict each other's story—just as it happened at the time. The book is also a visual portrait of the period. All the material was written or spoken or photographed by Americans, about themselves— it is the 1930's uninhibited by historical hindsight.

I hope this book will serve to document the period, a very special one indeed, in a way that has immediacy and provides new insight. Creating it has opened up for me a wonderful time-warp, which I hope the reader will now share.
SUSAN WINSLOW

We in America today are nearer to the final triumph over poverty than ever before in the history of any land. The poor-house is vanishing from among us. Herbert Hoover; 1928

# THE SCENE OF THE CRASH

October 24, 1929

**STOCKS OFF 5 BILLION IN SEVEREST BREAK IN WALL ST. HISTORY**

The stock market was shaken to its foundations yesterday by the severest break in the history of Wall Street. The immediate cause of the debacle, which was entirely unexpected, was the forced liquidation of large brokerage accounts and furious bear attacks that chopped from $5,000,000,000 to $7,000,000,000 in values from shares. Trading on the floor of the Stock Exchange was virtually paralyzed . . .

The zero hour came around 2 p.m. when the choicest issues on the list, along with the weakest, were smashed with a fury that the oldest traders in Wall Street confessed was without precedent . . .

Extreme losses were the order of the day, but banking and brokerage interests could look on imperturbably, because, anomalous as it may seem, it was considered in most circles that the stock market was functioning as a separate phenomenon, without effect on or relation to the economic and financial system of the country. A speculative mirage, grown to towering proportions since last summer, was merely being dispelled, leaving the familiar outlines of the world of reality unchanged.

*New York Herald Tribune*

October 25, 1929

Huge crowds in a holiday mood, resembling a confetti of faces from the upper stories of Wall Street skyscrapers, surged up and down the narrow streets of the financial district yesterday in search of excitement, and found it aplenty.

Brokerage houses were jammed with anxious tape watchers and the floors of the Stock and Curb Exchanges were in an uproar . . .

Newsboys, out-of-town visitors, housewives, truck drivers, teamsters, longshoremen from the nearby docks, bus conductors and collegians were in the daytime crowd hoping to see a World Series of finance enacted before their eyes. Prosaic truth was disregarded. Wild rumors were taken as gospel.

Baseless rumors about the failure of the Stock Exchange houses, banks and large speculators were considered with bated breath and further excited the curious throng, which ran from street to street at the slightest excuse. The appearance of a crowd of newsboys with extras was the cue for more running and shouting . . .

Around the Stock Exchange and the offices of J. P. Morgan & Co. the crowds were especially heavy and extra police from the Old Slip station were called out to handle the situation . . .

Persons bruised by the rough milling brought ambulances clanging into Wall Street, and more rumors were started about the collapse of traders on the floor of the Exchange.

A great deal of consideration was given by the street spectators to reports that six traders had been carried from the Stock Exchange on stretchers. The sudden illness of some one in a law office, not a market operator, brought an ambulance down Broad Street and started rumors that a trader, caught in the market, had jumped from a window.

From then on reports were frequent that brokers and others had jumped from windows . . .

Other features of the day that made Wall Street take on the psychology of a mining camp included the renting of all available rooms in hotels along the Brooklyn waterfront late in the afternoon by brokers who felt it necessary to keep close to the scene of the action. Whole floors were rented for employees who needed some sleep before the opening at 10 o'clock today.

One hotel placed a hundred extra beds and cots in hallways and parlors to help solve the sudden housing problem, created by workers who were too busy to go to their homes.

All crowd records, both for day and night, were broken, old-timers in Wall Street asserted . . .

The turmoil in the street was scarcely heeded by spectators who had lost fortunes and who crowded the offices of their brokers. Many wept unrestrainedly and some kicked over the tickers in a rage, throwing scores of tickers out of commission by breaking wire circuits . . .

All the telephone wires in lower Manhattan were busy throughout the day and phone exchanges were unable to cope with the unusual amount of business that developed as soon as the market opened. Traders who had had no intention of going downtown were forced to do so in order to keep in touch with the situation, being unable to get their brokerage houses on the telephone.

Brokerage houses, both uptown and downtown, were hushed, in contrast to the usual noise. People seemed to be moving around on tiptoe, unwilling to add to the disturbance of the stock market and unable for a time to believe what was happening to prices.

*New York Herald Tribune*


Believing that the fundamental conditions of the country are sound and that there is nothing in the business situation to warrant the destruction of values that has taken place on the exchanges during the past week, my son and I have for some days been purchasing sound common stocks. We are continuing and will continue our purchases in substantial amounts, at levels which we believe represent sound investment values.

John D. Rockefeller, Sr.; October 30, 1929

## RIORDAN A MARKET SUICIDE

The suicide of James J. Riordan, president of the County Trust Company, financial backer of the Democratic Party, and close friend of former Gov. Alfred E. Smith, was revealed early yesterday afternoon—almost 24 hours after Riordan shot himself.

The banker, who was 47, was a victim of the stock market. He died with a bullet through his right temple in his bedroom at the home of his sister, Mrs. Margaret Murray, at 21 West 12th Street, where he lived, on Friday afternoon . . .

Both Mrs. Murray and Mrs. [Molly] Geagan, [the maid], told the medical examiner that Riordan had been depressed and in poor health for about 3 weeks and that for several days he was not in a normal mental state.

The banker is reported to have suffered heavily in the collapse of Radio shares. Radio dropped to $35\frac{1}{2}$ on Friday, a loss of $14\frac{1}{2}$ points . . .

News of the suicide broke like a bomb yesterday at the National Democratic Club during a luncheon given by the Democratic Union attended by Gov. Franklin D. Roosevelt, Lieut. Gov. Herbert Lehman and John F. Curry, sachem of Tammany Hall.

The luncheon was postponed and the guests, all friends of Riordan's, left the table and divided into little knots, discussing the tragedy. Gov. Roosevelt, seemingly profoundly shocked, only murmured: 'This is terrible; this is terrible.'

*New York Sunday News*; November 10, 1929

New York City

Some reassuring utterance by the President of the United States . . . would do much to restore the confidence of the people.
William Randolph Hearst; November, 1929

Any lack of confidence in the economic future or the basic strength of business in the United States is foolish.
Herbert Hoover; November, 1929

## No Men Wanted

With assets of perhaps twenty dollars and some nine years' experience as a reporter in New England I came to New York to find a job. The round of newspaper offices and news bureaus netted me a series of polite but firm statements to the effect that 'there's nothing open just now, but you might leave your name and address.' After two weeks of this I set myself to what I believed would be the much easier task of securing a clerical place, or even something like ushering in a theatre, 'hopping the bells' at a hotel, or running an elevator in an office building.

Innocently enough, I followed the crowd to the agencies on Sixth Avenue. Visions of being sent to a position where a percentage would be taken from the first month's salary for a fee were quickly dissolved in the face of the cold fact that any position must be paid for in full and in advance. I learned from one young man that he had paid $10 for a job at which he had worked only four days, receiving $13.50, or a net profit of $3.50 for his four days of work. He and other victims told me, apparently from experience, that many of the agencies made a regular practice of sending men to jobs for which they were obviously unsuited, so that the same job might be sold several times. Many of the men, I learned, realized this, but were willing to 'take a gypping' in order to earn a few dollars.

My funds were getting low, and rather than spend any more of the bit of cash I still had I resolved to ride the subways for the night. Not only did I find this fairly easy, I found that hundreds of others were doing it. Experts at the game—men who live a hand-to-mouth existence by panhandling and petty racketeering—told me that the most satisfactory system was to ride the B.M.T. trains which run from Times Square to Coney Island, swinging around a loop and returning. This trip consumes nearly two hours if a local train is taken. A good corner seat gives the rider a chance to get a fair nap, and the thing can be repeated endlessly. When morning came I went to the Grand Central Terminal, where I washed for a nickel.

Sleeping in the parks, I found, was much less satisfactory than the comfort offered by the rapid-transit companies. Tired, hungry, and cold, I stretched out on the bench, and despite the lack of downy mattress and comforter eventually fell asleep. The soles of my feet were swollen with blisters, because my shoes had not been removed in at least seventy-two hours and I had tramped the sidewalks for three days . . .

Finally, I stood in the breadline in Twenty-fifth Street, where the women's section of the Socialist Party daily distributed soup, coffee, and bread. To my surprise, I found in the line all types of men—the majority being skilled craftsmen unable to find work. One of them told me he had been a civil engineer and had earned $8,000 a year. Since losing his job almost a year ago, he had drifted from bad to worse, occasionally picking up odd jobs, until he had sunk to the breadline. The professional bums usually found in such a place were conspicuously lacking. True, there were several unemployables—men

13

in the sixties, who stood no chance in competition with the thousands of younger, healthier men. There were also a number of middle-aged men who had long since given up the idea of finding work. Having started honestly enough in a sincere effort to get placed, they had met disappointment so consistently that their ambition was broken. Now, their attitude was expressed in the philosophical comment one of them made to me: 'Why should I work? I'm living along on one charity and another.' Such men never think of the future in terms of more than one or two days . . .

[But] there are many men who still hope despite months of failure. Of a dozen men in the park of nights, at least eight will tell you that they have something in mind for the following day, and they actually convince themselves. A few nights later a casual search will reveal the same men, still with 'something in mind for tomorrow.' For most of them that tomorrow is many months ahead. Perhaps it will never

come. In the meantime, they read, under the arc light in the park, in second-hand newspapers, predictions that business will be normal again in sixty days.
**No Men Wanted**; Karl Monroe; *Nation*; 1930

I see nothing in the present situation that is either menacing or warrants pessimism. During the winter months there may be some slackness or unemployment, but hardly more than at this season each year. I have every confidence that there will be a revival of activity in the Spring and that during the coming year the country will make steady progress.
Secretary of the Treasury Andrew W. Mellon; January, 1930

### The Daring Young Man on the Flying Trapeze
He (the living) dressed and shaved, grinned at himself in the mirror. Very unhandsome, he said; where is my tie? (he had but one.) Coffee and a gray sky, Pacific Ocean fog, the drone of a passing street car, people going to the city, time again, the day, prose and poetry.
He moved swiftly down the stairs to the street and began to walk . . .
Helplessly his mind sang, *He flies through the air with the greatest of ease, the daring young man on the flying trapeze*; then laughed with all the might of his being. It was really a splendid morning: gray, cold, and cheerless, a morning for inward vigour; ah, Edgar Guest, he said, how I long for your music.

In the gutter, he saw a coin which proved to be a penny dated 1923, and placing it in the palm of his hand he examined it closely, remembering the year and thinking of Lincoln, whose profile was stamped on the coin. There was almost nothing a man could do with a penny. I will purchase a motor-car, he thought. I will dress myself in the fashion of a fop, visit the hotel strumpets, drink and dine, and then return to the quiet. Or I will drop the coin in a slot and weigh myself.

It was good to be poor, and the Communists—but it was dreadful to be hungry. What appetites they had, how fond they were of food! Empty stomachs. He remembered how greatly he needed food. Every meal was bread and coffee and cigarettes, and now he had no more bread. Coffee without bread could never honestly serve as supper, and there were no weeds in the park that could be cooked as spinach is cooked.

If the truth were known, he was half starved, and there was still no end of books he ought to read before he died . . . He thought earnestly, I ought at least to read Hamlet once again; or perhaps Huckleberry Finn.

It was then that he became thoroughly awake; at the thought of dying. Now wakefulness was a state in the nature of a sustained shock. A young man could perish rather unostentatiously, he thought . . . Water and prose were fine, they filled much inorganic space, but they were inadequate. If there were only some work he might do for money, some trivial labor in the name of commerce. If they would only allow him to sit at a desk all day and add trade figures, subtract and multiply and divide, then perhaps he would not die. He would buy food, all sorts of it: untasted delicacies from Norway, Italy, and France; all manners of beef, lamb, fish, cheese, grapes, figs, pears, apples, melons, which he would worship when he had satisfied his hunger. He would place a bunch of red grapes on a dish beside two black figs, a large yellow pear, and a green apple. He would hold a cut melon to his nostrils for hours. He would buy great brown loaves of French bread, vegetables of all sorts, meat, life . . .

*Through the air on a flying trapeze*, his mind hummed. Amusing it was, astoundingly funny. A trapeze to God, or to nothing, a flying trapeze to some sort of eternity; he prayed objectively for strength to be able to make the flight with grace.

I have one cent, he said. It is an American coin. In the evening, I shall polish it until it glows like a sun and I shall study the words . . .

He went to the large department stores: there was a good deal of pomposity, some humiliation on his part, and finally the report that work was not available. He did not feel displeased, and strangely did not even feel that he was personally involved in all the foolishness. He was a living young man who was in need of money with which to go on being one, and there was no way of getting it except by working for it; and there was no work. It was purely an abstract problem which he wished for the last time to attempt to solve . . .

In the Civic Center Park, across from the Public Library Building, he drank almost a quart of water and felt himself refreshed. An old man was standing in the centre of the brick boulevards surrounded by sea-gulls, pigeons, and robins. He was taking handfuls of bread crumbs from a large paper sack and tossing them to the birds with a gallant gesture.

Dimly he felt impelled to ask the old man for a portion of the crumbs, but would not allow the thought even nearly to reach consciousness; he entered the Public Library and for an hour read Proust, then, feeling himself to be swimming away . . . he rushed outdoors. He drank more water at the fountain in the park and began the long walk to his room . . . He reached his room early in the afternoon and immediately prepared coffee on the small gas-range. There was no milk in the can, and the half pound of sugar he had purchased a week before was all gone; he drank a cup of the hot black fluid, sitting on his bed and smiling . . .

He began to polish the penny he had found in the morning, and this absurd act somehow afforded him great enjoyment. No American coin can be made to shine so brilliantly as a penny. How many pennies would he need to go on living? Wasn't there something more he might sell? He looked about the bare room. No . . .

He placed the shining penny on the table, looking upon it with the delight of a miser. How prettily it smiles, he said. Without reading them, he looked at the words, E PLURIBUS UNUM ONE CENT UNITED STATES OF AMERICA, and turning the penny over, he saw Lincoln and the words, IN GOD WE TRUST LIBERTY 1923. How beautiful it is, he said.

He became drowsy and felt a ghastly illness coming over his blood, a feeling of nausea and disintegration. Bewildered, he stood beside his bed, thinking *there is nothing to do but sleep*. Already he felt himself making great strides through the fluid of the earth, swimming away to the beginning. He fell face down upon the bed, saying, I ought first at least to give the coin to some child. A child could buy any number of things with a penny.

Then swiftly, neatly, with the grace of the young man on the trapeze, he was gone from his body. For an eternal moment he was all things at once: the bird, the fish, the rodent, the reptile, and man. An ocean of print undulated endlessly and darkly before him. The city burned. The herded crowd rioted. The earth circled away, and knowing that he did so, he turned his lost face to the empty sky and became dreamless, unalive, perfect.

**The Daring Young Man on the Flying Trapeze**; William Saroyan; 1934

**Left: Bryant Park, New York City. Below: Breadline funded by Al Capone, Chicago**

There was a bunch of us in the men's room in the railroad station. A couple of guys were trying to sleep on the benches. There was an old drunk who looked as if he'd had a couple of cuspidors emptied on him. I leaned against a radiator. After a while a couple of cops came in. One of 'em said: 'All right, boys, break it up! Break it up!' and began pushing the guys out. I beat it into the can. I was pretty cold and wanted to stick around. One of the cops came in. I stood over a latrine. He stood behind me. After a while he said: 'Okeh, bud, long enough, you've broken all the records already.' I had to laugh at that. I buttoned my pants and went out of the station. I began walking again.

She was sitting on the stoop. When I walked by she crossed her legs showing her thighs and winked. I walked over to her. She said: 'How about it, hon?' I said: 'Christ, kid, if I had any dough I'd rather eat.' . . .

You get shoved out early; you get your coffee and start walking. A couple of hours before noon you get in line. You eat and start walking. At night you flop where you can. You don't talk. You eat what you can. You sleep where you can. You walk. No one talks to you. You walk. It's cold, and you shiver and stand in doorways or sit in railroad stations. You don't see much. You forget. You walk an hour and forget where you started from. It is day, and then it's night, and then it's day again. And you don't remember which was first. You walk. There are men with fat on them and you know it. There are lean men and you know it.

**On the Move**; M. Shulimson; *New Masses*; January 23, 1934

These really are good times but only a few know it.
Henry Ford; March, 1930

**Turpentine worker's family, Alabama**

In any consideration of the general problem of unemployment the Negro is apt to be forgotten. It is assumed that inevitably a large number of Negroes are out of a job; it remains for a sober, unhysterical organization like the National Urban League to come forward and show that the percentage of Negroes among the unemployed runs sometimes four, five, six times as high as their population percentage warrants. This is especially true, of course, in the industrial areas, and a careful study of the question indicates that the percentage of Negro unemployed runs higher in the Northern industrial centers where the Negro is limited to unskilled occupations, where he is in fact the marginal worker.

The preponderance of Negro unemployed is due to a number of causes. Obviously, in almost any community, when jobs are scarce preference is given to the white worker in case of a vacancy; but worse than this, a fairly widespread tendency is observed to replace Negro workers with white. White girls have replaced Negro waiters, hotel workers, elevator operators, of course at reduced wages; Filipinos have replaced Negro men under the same conditions. In the drought-affected areas of the Southwest, Negroes, stripped of their livelihood, have drifted to the cities—and found nothing there. Finally, there is considerable evidence that in the jobs specially created to ameliorate the difficulties of the depression—for example, in public works— Negroes find it much harder to get work than whites . . .

The economic structure of the Negro race, as a result, is in an alarming state of threatened disintegration. The effect of such a disintegration upon the whites is obvious, and the unsettled state of the color question is reflected in the increased number of lynchings. If we are not careful, the present economic depression will put the solution of the Negro problem back many years.

**Negroes out of Work**; *Nation*; April 22, 1931

The average man won't really do a day's work unless he is caught and cannot get out of it. There is plenty of work to do, if people would do it.

Henry Ford; March, 1931

There is not an unemployed man in the country that hasn't contributed to the wealth of every millionaire in America. The working classes didn't bring this on, it was the big boys that thought the financial drunk was going to last forever, and overbought, overmerged and overcapitalized . . .

We got more wheat, more corn, more food, more cotton, more money in the banks, more everything in the world than any nation that ever lived ever had, yet we are starving to death. We are the first nation in the history of the world to go to the poorhouse in an automobile.

Will Rogers; November, 1931

**A School Principal**: 'We were practicing for a chorus and a little boy about twelve was in the front line. All at once he pitched forward in a dead faint. This was two o'clock in the afternoon . . . He said he was hungry. He had not had anything to eat since the day before.'

**An Unemployed Man**: 'I have two boys to go to work. They haven't any shoes, no clothes. They can't go to look for a job because they haven't any shoes.'

**A Charity Worker**: 'One woman said, "If I could only have just one meal that my husband has bought, the food would taste so much better!" '

**An Unemployed Man**: 'I plugged in and got gas. I have stolen coal. You may wonder how that has affected my mind.'

**Another**: 'If I were honest it would be a sin not a virtue, inasmuch as it would deprive my children of food.'

Chicago Workers' Committee on Unemployment Report; 1932

We can say with satisfaction of this period of nearly twenty months of continuous economic degeneration that we have had fewer strikes and lockouts than in normal times; that we have had no mob violence worth noting to trouble the police or the militia; we have not summoned a single Federal soldier to arms . . . With only local and unnecessary exceptions there has been no starvation . . . The first duty of the Government—that is, to secure social tranquillity and to maintain confidence in our institutions—has been performed.

Herbert Hoover; May, 1931

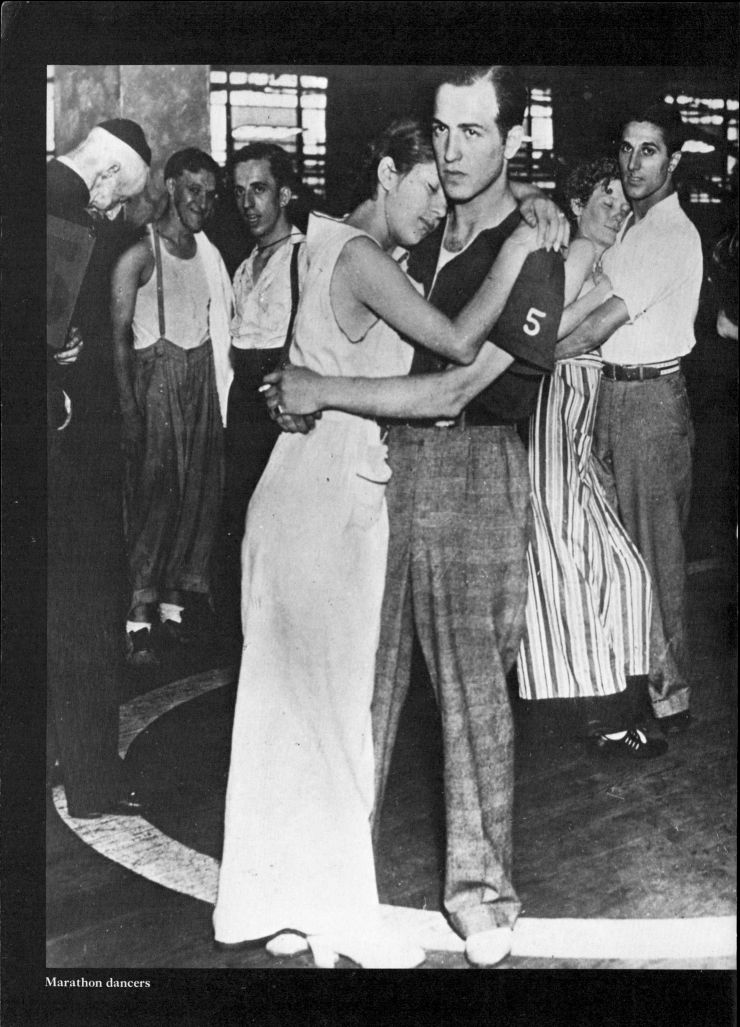

Marathon dancers

How happy to be an American,
  One of the chosen breed,
Who live in a land of abundance,
  Where no one is ever in need.
As long as a man is willing to work
  He is bound to get on well,
And there are two chickens in every pot—
  There are, like Hell!

How happy to be a dweller
  In the land of the Brave and the Free,
Where Special Privilege is Unknown
  And there's Opportunity!
Here Equal Distribution of Wealth
  Spreads calm contentment's spell,
And there are two cars in every garage—
  There are, like Hell!

How happy to live in the U.S.A.
  From crime and violence free,
Where gangs and rackets never disturb
  Public security!
Where the gilded rewards of a life of shame
  Never tempt Our Nell,
For the working girl makes more than the tart—
  She does, like Hell!

How happy to be a citizen
  Where the voice of the people rules,
Where there are no grafters in office,
  Nor corporation tools;
Where justice, the right of everyman,
  No one can buy and sell,
And the courts are the poor man's refuge—
  They are, like Hell!

How happy to be a free man
  In the land of mirth and cheer,
Where life floats gaily on rivers of wine
  And oceans of foaming beer.
No bigot troubles this favored land,
  No kill-joy here may dwell,
And personal freedom is unrestrained—
  It is, like Hell!

How happy to be a soldier
  Of the old Red, White and Blue
Paid like a banker in time of war,
  And cared for afterward too,
With a job and a home in the city
  Or a fertile farm in the dell,
For like Princes we treat our Veterans—
  We do, like Hell!

**The Happy American**; song; Anonymous; 1932

Smile away the Depression!

Smile us into Prosperity!
*wear a*
SMILETTE!

This wonderful little gadget will
solve the problems of the Nation!

APPLY NOW AT YOUR CHAMBER OF COMMERCE
OR THE REPUBLICAN NATIONAL COMMITTEE
WARNING—*Do not risk Federal arrest by looking glum!*

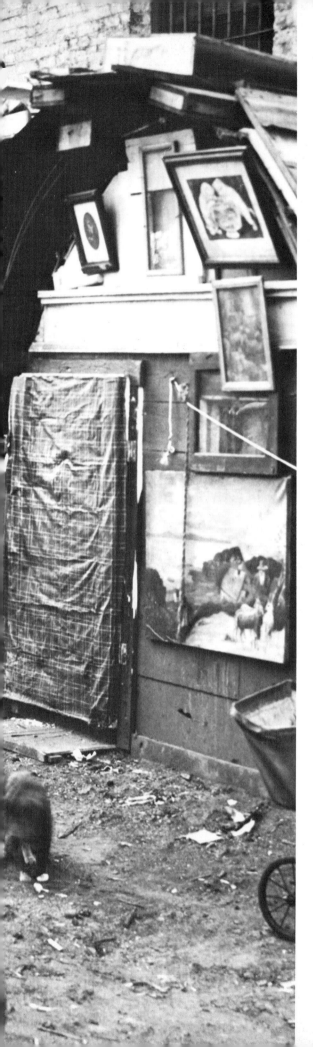

Left: New York City

Above: John D. Rockefeller, Sr.,
giving out dime

All the really important millionaires are planning to continue
prosperity.
Arthur Brisbane; November 26, 1929

# WHEN MR. HOOVER SAYS OKAY

Informal polls of the House of Representatives have created apprehension in the country that a further bonus bill of $2,000,000,000 or
thereabouts for World War veterans will be passed.

I wish to state again that I am absolutely opposed to any such
legislation . . .

Such action would undo every effort that is being made to reduce
government expenditures and balance the budget. The first duty of
every citizen of the United States is to build up and sustain the credit
of the United States government. Such an action would irretrievably
undermine it.

Herbert Hoover; March, 1932

A bunch of out-of-work ex-service men in Portland, Oregon, figured they needed their bonus now; 1945 would be too late, only buy wreaths for their tombstones. They figured out, too, that the bonus paid now would tend to liven up business, particularly the retail business in small towns; might be just enough to tide them over till things picked up. Anyway, everybody else was getting a bonus; the moratorium was a bonus to European nations, the R.F.C. was handing out bonuses to railroads and banks, how about the men who'd made the world safe for democracy getting their bonus, too? God knows we're the guys that need it worst. Every other interest has got lobbyists in Washington. It's up to us to go to Washington and be our own lobbyists. Park benches can't be any harder in Washington than they are back home.

So three hundred of them started east in old cars and trucks, hitchhiking, riding on freight trains . . . By the time they reached Council Bluffs [Iowa] they found that other groups all over the country were rebelling against their veterans' organizations and getting the same idea. It was an Army. They organized it as such and nicknamed it the B.E.F. [Bonus Expeditionary Force.]
**The Veterans Come Home to Roost**; John Dos Passos; *New Republic*; June, 1932

We're all the way from Oregon
To get some cash from Washington,
Hinkey, dinkey, parlez-vous.

East St. Louis, Ill. May 23, 1932
More than 300 World War veterans, on their way from Portland, Oregon to Washington to urge passage of the bonus bill by Congress, remained 'camped' in the Baltimore & Ohio railroad yards here tonight, blocked by refusal of the railroad to move the freight train which they had boarded today for the rest of their journey.

The train was scheduled to leave at mid-afternoon, but instead, some of the cars were disconnected and shunted back into the train sheds.
*New York Times*

We're going to ride the B & O.
The good Lord Jesus told us so.
Hinkey, dinkey, parlez-vous.

[By June 7th,] eight thousand men and more had already reached the capital. Their ranks on this warm night showed many things—what ten years of life in prosperous America had done . . .

Some of the men wore empty bean cans strapped to their belts, for water. They *wore* them lest some covetous friends steal them; empty bean cans were hard to find. A man may be known by his treasures— or at least, by the measure of his need.

So they made for America a picture of honest men in poverty. If the B.E.F. had been evicted on the morrow one of its chief functions would have been accomplished. For Mr. Hoover had said there were no hungry men in America. Either he was wrong or these men imagined their hunger.
**B.E.F.: The Whole Story of the Bonus Army**; W. W. Waters; 1933

You're going to see a better day
When Mr. Hoover says 'O.K.'
Hinkey, dinkey, parlez-vous.

Bonus Marchers in Washington,
summary 1932

Now they are camped on Anacostia Flats in the southeast corner of Washington. Nearly twenty thousand of them altogether. Everywhere you meet new ragged troops staggering in. A few have gone home discouraged, but very few. Anacostia Flats is the recruiting center; from there they are sent to new camps scattered around the outskirts of Washington. Anacostia Flats is a ghost of an army camp from the days of the big parade, with its bugle calls, its mess lines, greasy K.P.'s, M.P.'s, headquarters, liaison officers, a medical officer. Instead of the tents and the long tarpaper barracks of those days, the men are sleeping in little lean-tos built out of old newspapers, cardboard boxes, packing crates, bits of tin or tarpaper roofing, every kind of cockeyed makeshift shelter from the rain, scraped together out of the city dump.

The doughboys have changed, too, as well as their uniforms and housing, in these fifteen years. There's the same goulash of faces and dialects, foreigners' pidgin English, lingoes from industrial towns and farming towns, East, Northeast, Middle West, Southwest, South; but we were all youngsters then; now we are getting on into middle life, sunken eyes, hollow cheeks off breadlines, pale-looking knotted hands of men who've worked hard with them, and then for a long time have not worked.

**The Veterans Come Home to Roost**; John Dos Passos

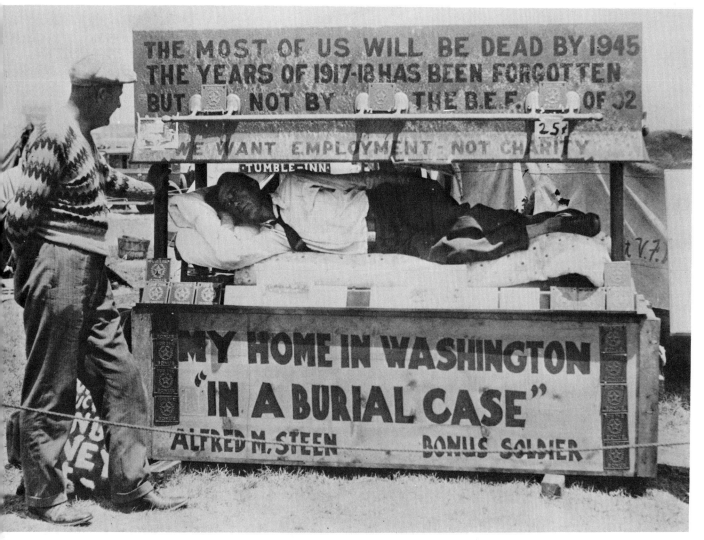

Last week the House of Representatives surrendered to the siege of
the Bonus Expeditionary Force encamped near the Capitol. It voted
(226–175) to take up the bill by Texas' Patman for immediate cashing
of the Adjusted Service Compensation certificates at a cost of
$2,400,000,000 in printing-press money. This first test of the Bonus
boosters' strength indicated that the House would probably pass the
bill and send it to the Senate. In that body 56 Senators—a majority—
were said to be lined up against the Bonus. But even should the
measure somehow get by Congress an insurmountable veto awaited
it at the White House . . .

Bonus lobbyists swarmed about the Capitol. One group
encountered Senator Lewis of Illinois in a corridor, pestered him for
support. Angry when his way was blocked, Senator Lewis declared:
'I'm going to the Senate and you can go to hell!'
*Time*; June 20, 1932

They used to tell me I was building a dream,
And so I followed the mob—
When there was earth to plow or guns to bear
I was always there—right on the job.
They used to tell me I was building a dream
With peace and glory ahead—
Why should I be standing on line
Just waiting for bread?

Once I built a railroad, made it run,
Made it race against time.
Once I built a railroad,
Now it's done—
Brother, can you spare a dime?
Once I built a tower, to the sun.
Brick and rivet and lime,
Once I built a tower,
Now it's done—
Brother, can you spare a dime?
Once in khaki suits,
Gee, we looked swell,
Full of that Yankee Doodle-de-dum.
Half a million boots went sloggin' through Hell,
I was the kid with the drum.
Say don't you remember, they called me Al—
It was Al all the time.
Say, don't you remember I'm your pal—
Buddy, can you spare a dime?

**Brother, Can You Spare a Dime?**
Song; Gorney and Harburg; 1932

**Walter W. Waters, B.E.F. Commander**

It was learned that while the Federal Government is ostensibly keeping hands off, it in reality is watching the situation very closely. From a high District official it was learned that the War Department was being kept informed of every detail of the situation. Both the soldiers and marines who are in the barracks near the city are being kept on the alert against any emergency caused by the presence of the great gathering of hungry and destitute men.

*New York Times*; June 11, 1932

'If the troops should be called out against us will the B.E.F. be given the opportunity to form in column, salvage their belongings, and retreat in an orderly fashion?'

   'Yes, my friend, of course!'

**B.E.F.** Commander W. W. Waters to General Douglas MacArthur, Army Chief of Staff

July 27, 1932

The Commissioners (of the District of Columbia) accept your plan to evacuate 200 men from the buildings they occupy (at Pennsylvania Ave. & 3rd St.) by six o'clock tomorrow evening.

Chief of D.C. Police Pelham Glassford to B.E.F. Commander W. W. Waters

At 9:30 on the morning of this Thursday, the 28th . . . I told the men who gathered in front [of a small building at 3rd St. & Pennsylvania Ave.] of my plan and hinted vaguely at the consequences if they did not follow it. There was plenty of booing from the crowd but I expected it. Some of it was 'planted' there. I knew however, that with the time the Commissioners had promised me, I could eventually persuade the men to leave and could get my daily quota out to Camp Bartlett.

Some of the men were sore. 'By God, Waters, have you lost your nerve?' 'How much did you get for selling out to Hoover?' 'What about 1945?' . . .

'You can sit there and by doing so jeopardize the lives of women and children,' I said. 'If troops do come you mugs will be the first ones to run. I've made an agreement which is the best thing for all of us, and you'll stick to it.'

Several men began to turn toward the building to gather up their belongings before moving. I was going to get 200 without difficulty. Suddenly there was a slight commotion in the crowd, caused, it seemed to me, by some of the men. I was wrong. A civilian was pushing his way through the crowd trying to get to me at the platform.

It was a Mr. Walker, General Glassford's secretary. I tried to guess what had brought him here but there was no need to guess. He handed me a slip of paper. It was an order from the Treasury Department, calling for the complete evacuation of this building—by ten o'clock on this morning!

The promise of the Commissioners ——!

Ten minutes to get the men out! If ever a group was trying to start trouble, so as to take advantage of it, the forces of Government were doing their best to egg on the men of the B.E.F. into some sort of riot.

B.E.F.; W. W. Waters

Treasury agents arrived at 10 am to clear the buildings. Most of the veterans refused to leave. Police helped the Federal men do their job. Hundreds of veterans swelled to thousands as men flocked from other B.E.F. camps to the scene to watch the eviction. By noon the buildings had been practically cleared when a trio of veterans carrying a US flag tried to march back in. Police blocked them. Somebody tossed a brick. 'There's a fight!' went up the cry. More bricks flew.

'Give the cops hell!' a veteran shouted. His massed companions pressed upon the police, now flailing with their clubs. The fighting spread with quick contagion. One policeman had his head bashed in. Veterans trampled him. Blood streamed down others' faces. Veterans swung scrap iron, hunks of concrete, old boards. General Glassford rushed into the mêlée, was knocked flat by a brick. Before he could get up, a veteran snatched off his gold police badge.

Time; August 8, 1932

Washington, July 28, 1932

The arrival of Federal agents might in itself have been sufficient inflammatory material to start the blaze. Now they were gone and nothing had happened. Then filtering through the crowd I began to see members from the Communist camp. The second batch of inflammatory material had arrived, the best and truest allies the Administration had in stirring up trouble . . .

The Reds, carrying an American flag, reached the police lines and, although they had no business behind them, tried to break through. The police grappled with them. Bricks, and there were thousands lying around, flew through the air. For about six minutes the fight continued, twenty police against forty veterans, most of them, 'Reds.' . . .

Then General Glassford managed to reach a vantage point and called, 'How about let's stopping for lunch?' The riot stopped. The General had been in the middle of it and during the fight, some Communist had grabbed at the badge on his shirt and had torn it off. Two men of the B.E.F. knocked the 'Red' down, got the badge back, and handed it to the General.

As I came up to the fight I saw one of the men in the front line, who had started the rioting, move back, run off the lot, and enter a car that started away immediately. There have been plenty of rumors that the riot was really started by the Administration; and one of the Treasury employees, so I am told, has been missing ever since the day of that riot.

**That rioting was all that took place anywhere in Washington during this entire day!**
B.E.F.; W. W. Waters

When war came in 1917 William Hushka, 22-year-old Lithuanian, sold his St. Louis butcher shop, gave the proceeds to his wife, joined the Army. He was sent to Camp Funston, Kan. where he was naturalized. Honorably discharged in 1919, he drifted to Chicago, worked as a butcher, seemed unable to hold a steady job. His wife divorced him, kept their small daughter. Long jobless, in June he joined a band of veterans marching to Washington to fuse with the Bonus Expeditionary Force. 'I might as well starve there as here,' he told his brother. At the capital he was billeted in a Government-owned building on Pennsylvania Avenue. One of the thousands, he took part in the demonstration at the Capitol the day Congress adjourned without voting immediate cashing of the Bonus.

Last week William Hushka's Bonus for $528 suddenly became payable in full when a police bullet drilled him dead in the worst public disorder the capital has known in years.
*Time*; August 8, 1932

July 29, 1932
It was about 2 o'clock when the argument that culminated in the shooting occurred.

Two veterans engaged in an altercation in front of the camp supply building, and were immediately surrounded by a howling mob of about 100. Police rushed to the scene and sought to stop the argument. Gen. Glassford, with two policemen at his heels, ran up the stairway along the side of the building to the second floor to get a better view of the trouble. They were immediately followed by about 30 veterans who rushed the stairs and treated Glassford's two aides roughly when they sought to stop the rush.

About this time bricks started flying between groups down on the ground.

Officer George W. Shinault, on the outskirts of the milling mob, near the foot of the stairway, was getting a beating from the veterans. Bricks were flying about him. He drew his pistol and fired . . . Officer Miles Zamenaciack, who was on the second floor with Glassford, rushed halfway down the stairs and joined in the shooting. A third policeman, J. O. Fife, who was in the midst of the brick fighting on the ground, drew his pistol and started running toward the rear of the building, whence most of the people were coming. About 25 feet from Fife a bonus marcher drew back to hurl a brickbat at him, and, holding his pistol in both hands, Fife fired several times.
*Washington Evening Star*

At two o'clock General Glassford and a small group of police returned. They went to a large vacant building next to the one where the eviction had occurred in the morning. They started up a flight of stairs from the outside, intending to go to a top floor and to get a bird's-eye view of the scene. General Glassford led the way and a few policemen followed. A small group of veterans, curious, pushing and crowding, followed them closely. The crowd pressed behind them.

Suddenly, without warning, frightened perhaps by the pressure of the following veterans, the last man in the police line whirled about. His gun was in his hand. He fired straight at the veterans behind him and hit the first man. Twice more this policeman, Shinault, pulled the trigger. The policeman in front of him drew his gun, too, and fired one shot, and another veteran dropped, clutching his stomach.

A voice from the top of the stairs cried: 'Put down that gun!' It was General Glassford. Shinault whirled around at the sound of the voice. He pointed his gun directly at the General for a moment then, sheepishly, as if caught in some harmless boyish prank, put the gun in his holster.

Not a veteran had threatened him. But two of their number lay silent on the ground and their blood toned the red of the pile of brick dust. Over the entire crowd of milling veterans spread silence . . . There was no rioting, no brick throwing, no protest—just silence in the face of murder . . .

Five days later we were to bury William Hushka, the first man shot. He had been recruited for the B.E.F. out of a breadline in Chicago. Seven days later we were to bury Eric Carlson, the second victim.
B.E.F.; W. W. Waters

July 28, 1932

The President:

The Commissioners of the District of Columbia regret to inform you that during the past few hours, circumstances of a serious character have arisen in the District of Columbia which have been the cause of unlawful acts of large numbers of so-called 'Bonus Marchers,' who have been in Washington for some time past.

This morning officials of the Treasury Department, seeking to clear certain areas within the Government triangle in which there were numbers of these Bonus Marchers, met with resistance. They called upon the Metropolitan Police force for assistance and a serious riot occurred. Several members of the Metropolitan Police were injured, one reported seriously. The total number of Bonus Marchers greatly outnumber the police, the situation is made more difficult by the fact that this area contains thousands of brickbats and these were used by the rioters in their attack upon the police.

Federal troops assemble on Washington Bridge

In view of the above, it is the opinion of the Major and Superintendent of Police, in which the Commissioners concur, that it will be impossible for the Police Department to maintain law and order except by the free use of firearms, which will make the situation a dangerous one; it is believed, however, that the presence of Federal troops in some number will obviate the seriousness of the situation and result in far less violence and bloodshed.

The Commissioners of the District of Columbia therefore request that they be given the assistance of Federal troops in maintaining law and order in the District of Columbia.

Very sincerely yours,
L. H. Reichelderfer
President, Board of Commissioners of the District of Columbia

General Douglas MacArthur
Chief of Staff, U.S. Army                                    2.50pm July 28, 1932

You will have United States troops proceed immediately to the scene of disorder. Cooperate fully with the District of Columbia police force which is now in charge. Surround the affected area and clear it without delay.

Turn over all prisoners to the civil authorities.

In your orders insist that any women or children who may be in the affected area be afforded every consideration and kindness. Use all humanity consistent with the due execution of the order.

Patrick J. Hurley, Secretary of War
July 28, 1932

MacArthur has decided to go into active command in the field.
General Douglas MacArthur to Major Dwight D. Eisenhower

**General Douglas MacArthur**

July 29, 1932

The troops first took up position south of the White House on the Ellipse, and just after 4:30 p.m. marched down Pennsylvania Avenue to the affected area . . .

After a brief conference between police and Army officials, the cavalrymen, with drawn sabers, were ordered to drive back the thousands of onlookers. A 14-year-old boy suffered a saber cut on the arm in the process.

After the crowd had been driven back several blocks, a detachment of infantry laid aside their rifles and donned gas masks.

One group approached the front of a partly demolished building in which a large number of veterans were housed, and hurled a dozen tear gas bombs. The veterans were driven out through the rear of the building and were met by a second barrage of tear gas. Under this second attack, they retreated from the area . . .

After policemen had hauled down and folded up some American flags waving over the crudely constructed veterans' shelters, infantry-men with long flaming brands in their hands went from hut to hut and tent to tent leaving behind them flame and ruin . . .

Behind a towering colored man carrying an American flag, a group of bonus marchers surged across the street between two of the cavalrymen who were holding the line.

The man, dressed in riding boots and trousers, held the flag aloft and threw his head back shouting he would not move. He was the point of a triangle behind which a hundred or more of the marchers quickly grouped themselves.

After the cavalrymen had tried unavailingly to push the man back, all but planting their horses' feet upon him, they gave up that gesture and put their horses squarely into the crowd, five of them breaking pell mell through and literally throwing the flag bearer and his followers back on the pavement beyond the flying hoofs of the horses . . .

The troops laid their second gas attack on the small bonus camp near Four-and-a-half St. and Maryland Avenue, southwest . . . Here the first casualty among the troops occurred when Corporal K. Quick of Ft. Myer was struck in the head with a brick . . .

The Cavalry charged the encampment, advancing under cover of tear gas and were met by a volley of bricks hurled by the veterans. They used the flats of their sabers freely in pushing the crowd back into line . . . The veterans, used to the gas by this time, began throwing the bombs back at the soldiers . . .

Headed by Gen. MacArthur, the troops began moving on the main bonus camp at Anacostia.

Exclaiming, 'I don't want any more bloodshed,' W. W. Waters 'commander' of the bonus army, circulated through the huge encampment seeking to have the veterans evacuate peacefully . . .

The offensive against the camp was launched at 10:09 by infantry-men with drawn bayonets, who hurled tear gas bombs into the crowd . . .

With their horses at a walk, the Cavalry went down the steep embankment into the camp area, followed immediately by [more] infantrymen, who set fire to a number of huts after first making sure every human had been cleared out . . .

After the troopers began applying torches, the veterans caught the idea and set fire to their own shacks. Twisting tongues of flame rose to a dense pall of black smoke. Under it, sharply etched against the flame glare, the soldiers advanced, the veterans retreated . . .

The whole camp was a mass of flames by 11 o'clock . . . The great camp was destroyed last night almost to the last shelter.

The Infantry went ahead with bayonets fixed, throwing tear gas bombs in place of hand grenades. The Cavalry came in at a charge, mostly relying on their mounts to scatter the veterans. Tanks were deployed and machine guns were in position, but the unarmed 'enemy' force did not require the use of the deadlier weapons . . .

Hundreds of Washingtonians crowded about got more than one whiff of tear gas while taking in the spectacle of a lifetime.

The women of the B.E.F., scores of them, with their children, sought new shelter. Some were hurried off to the Salvation Army quarters and charitable homes. One mother made a heart-tugging spectacle as she laid her small brood of three to sleep on a hard pavement. They slumbered soundly.

As the night wore on bewildered groups of the veterans, carrying blanket rolls and other meager possessions, wandered about in the street in the vicinity of the burning shacks . . . Everywhere was the penetrating smell of burning cloth and unsalvaged bedding.

Ambulances clung to the edge of the conflict and carried off men with battered heads, with eyes streaming from unbearable doses of the tear gas, and with all the other injuries that inevitably accompany civil disorder and its suppression.

*Washington Evening Star*

A challenge to the authority of the United States Government has been met, swiftly and firmly. After months of patient indulgence, the Government met overt lawlessness as it always must be met if the cherished processes of self-government are to be preserved. We cannot tolerate the abuse of Constitutional rights by those who would destroy all government, no matter who they may be. Government cannot be coerced by mob rule.

Herbert Hoover; July 28, 1932

**Overleaf: Bonus Marcher and family after burning of camp by troops**

Under the circumstances but two courses were left open to the President. One was to acquiesce in the violence and surrender the government to the mob. The other was to uphold law and order and suppress the mob.
Secretary of War Patrick Hurley; August 2, 1932

'Only two courses were open,
    As anyone can see:
To vindicate law and order
    Or yield to anarchy.'
Granted!—the Chiefs of Government
    Cannot tolerate mobs—
But isn't it strange you never thought
    Of giving the workless jobs?

'Only two courses were open'—
    When men who had fought for you
Starved in the streets of our cities,
    Finding no work to do—
When in the richest of the countries
    Babies wept unfed—
Strange it never occurred to you
    To give the hungry bread!

'Only two courses were open'—
    To the Higher Racketeers
Who look on human suffering
    With lofty well-fed sneers.
And thus will your names be noted
    By history's merciless pen:
'They knew how to rise to Power,
    But not how to act like Men!'
Song; Anonymous; 1932

# DR. NEW DEAL

In my calm judgment, the nation faces today a more grave emergency than in 1917.

It is said that Napoleon lost the Battle of Waterloo because he forgot his infantry. He staked too much upon the more spectacular but less substantial cavalry.

The present administration in Washington provides a close parallel. It has either forgotten or it does not want to remember the infantry of our economic army.

These unhappy times call for the building of plans that rest upon the forgotten, the unrecognized but the indispensable units of economic power, for plans like those of 1917 that build from the bottom up and not from the top down, that put their faith once more in the forgotten man at the bottom of the economic pyramid.

Franklin D. Roosevelt; April 8, 1932

**Previous pages: FDR, 1932 Presidential campaign. Above: with son James and Will Rogers at Democratic Convention in Chicago**

The national party convention is not only a time-honored piece of the machinery of government but a festival of the national religion. But whatever its value as ritual and spectacle, its primary purpose is the selection of a man to govern the country and the formulation of the policies that are needed for the public good. From that point of view both conventions came pretty close to being national disasters . . .

The dreary dullness of the Republican gathering, unmatched in the memory of men who have been going to national conventions for forty years, was no more than might have been expected of a collection of mechanical robots operated by remote control from the White House. They did not enjoy their job but they had to do it, could do nothing else; their hope of success rested not in what they were doing but in what they expected the Democrats to do . . . After twelve years of Republican administration had brought us to the most dangerous situation since 1861, the Republican party declared boldly: 'This is no time to experiment.' That is not conservatism; it is sheer fossilization . . .

Even the unblushing Assistant Secretary Jahncke, advertizing Mr. Hoover at Independence Hall on July 4th as the hope of the world and 'the master statesman of the future,' did not dare to call him the master statesman of the present.

**The Collapse of Politics**; Elmer Davis; *Harper's Magazine*; September, 1932

Should my countrymen again place on me the responsibilities of high office I shall carry forward the work of reconstruction. I shall hope long before another four years have passed to see the world prosperous and at peace and every American home again in the sunshine of genuine progress and genuine prosperity. I shall seek to maintain untarnished and unweakened those fundamental traditions and principles upon which our Nation was founded and upon which it has grown. This is my pledge to the Nation and to Almighty God.'
Herbert Hoover; Republican Nomination Acceptance; August, 1932

The Democrats failed to perform their historic function of making things easy for the Republicans. Instead of getting into a long fight, they made a quick nomination—selecting, to be sure, the man who would probably make the weakest President of the dozen aspirants. But so far as could be seen at convention time he would make the strongest candidate; and it is a strong candidate, not a strong President, that politicians want. Whatever you may say against the Democratic nomination, it was at least a triumph of the popular will. Most of the delegates who voted for Roosevelt did so not because they wanted him but because they thought the folks back home wanted him. That the folks back home wanted him only because he was a Protestant gentleman with a famous name did not matter . . .

Uneasy second thoughts were fairly common the day after the nomination among men who had voted for Roosevelt with a whoop and hurrah the night before. He dissipated them by the brilliant stroke of his prompt appearance and acceptance speech; he looked so well and sounded so well that weary delegates paid little attention to what he said. Taking note, apparently, of the charges of straddling that had been flung at him, he promised to make his position clear; and he did—on the prohibition plank which the party had adopted by a vote of five to one. For the rest, you could not quarrel with a single one of his generalities; you seldom can. But what they mean (if anything) is known only to Franklin D. Roosevelt and his God.
**The Collapse of Politics**; Elmer Davis

I pledge you—I pledge myself to a new deal for the American people. Let us all here assembled constitute ourselves prophets of a new order of competence and of courage. This is more than a political campaign; it is a call to arms. Give me your help, not to win votes alone, but to win in this crusade to restore America to its own people.
Franklin D. Roosevelt; Democratic nomination acceptance; July 2, 1932

I am waging a war in this campaign—a frontal attack, an onset— against the Four Horsemen of the present Republican leadership: the Horsemen of Destruction, Delay, Deceit, and Despair. And the time has come for us to marshal this 'Black Horse Cavalry.'
First of all, the Horseman of Destruction: the embodiment of governmental policies so unsound, so inimical to true progress that it has left behind in its trail everywhere economic paralysis, industrial

chaos, poverty and suffering. You have heard that Horseman clattering down your streets.

Next comes the Horseman of Delay . . . There is no time for delay when we have been led by these people into the quicksand. There is no time for delay when nearly half our people cannot buy the bare necessities of life. There is no time for delay when eleven millions of honest, industrious and willing men and women are tramping the streets and roads of our nation looking for work. There is no time to wait when the prosperity and happiness of the country are at stake.

And we of the Democratic party will not wait!

Next in line is the third Horseman—the Horseman of Deceit. It is his purpose to cover the trail of the Horsemen of Destruction and Delay. He tells you things that are not true. He wears a mask. He attempts by misrepresentations and distortions of facts to blind your eyes, to destroy your sense of direction, and to paralyze your power of action. He carries a great shield to hide from you the ugly ruin and terror which his comrades have left in their wake.

Bringing up the rear is the fourth Horseman—the Horseman of Despair. He tells you that our government has no control over conditions that are handled from overseas. He tells you that economic conditions must work themselves out. He tries to close the door of hope in your face.

We Americans will rise from destruction; we Americans will conquer despair; we Americans are facing new things. With confidence we accept the promise of a New Deal.

Franklin D. Roosevelt; campaign speech; October, 1932

November 9, 1932

**ROOSEVELT WINNER IN LANDSLIDE!**

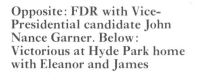
Opposite: FDR with Vice-Presidential candidate John Nance Garner. Below: Victorious at Hyde Park home with Eleanor and James

Happy days are here again!
The skies above are clear again!
Let's all sing a song of cheer again—
Happy days are here again!
**Happy Days Are Here Again**; FDR Campaign Song; 1932

**Giuseppe Zangara**

February 16, 1933

## ROOSEVELT ESCAPES NEW YORK ASSASSIN'S BULLET AT MIAMI; MAYOR CERMAK GRAVELY WOUNDED; FOUR OTHERS HIT

After I had finished speaking, someone from the talking-picture people climbed on the back of the car and said, 'You must repeat that speech for us.' I said I would not. He said, 'We have come 1,000 miles for this.' I said, 'I am very sorry, but I can't do it.'

Having said that, I slid off the back of the car into my seat.

Just then Mayor Cermak came forward and I talked with him about a minute about Chicago in general. Then he moved off behind the car. As he moved away a man came forward with a long telegram and started telling me what it contained. While he was talking I leaned forward. Just then I heard what I thought was a fire-cracker— then several more. The man talking with me pulled me back, and the chauffeur started the car.

I looked around and saw Mayor Cermak doubled up. I told the chauffeur to stop. He did, about fifteen feet from where we started. The Secret Service men shouted to him, 'Get out of the crowd.' The chauffeur started again, and I stopped him again—this time at the corner of the bandstand.

Looking back I saw Cermak being carried along, and we put him in our car. He was alive, but I was afraid he wouldn't last. I got my hand on his pulse and found none. He was on the seat with me, and I had my left arm around him. He slumped forward.

Then Cermak straightened up and I got his pulse. That was surprising. For three blocks I actually believed his heart had stopped.

I held him all the way to the hospital, and his pulse constantly improved. It seemed like twenty-five miles to the hospital.
Franklin D. Roosevelt, President-Elect; February 16, 1933

I do not know whether or not I shot Mr. Roosevelt, but I want to make it clear that I do not hate Mr. Roosevelt personally. I hate all Presidents, no matter from what country they come and I hate all officials and everybody who is rich . . . I'd kill every President, I'd kill them all.
Giuseppe Zangara; February 16, 1933

February 14, 1933

## EIGHT-DAY BANKING HOLIDAY IN MICHIGAN PROCLAIMED BY GOVERNOR IN 'EMERGENCY'

As in past waves of financial hysteria, the collapse of a leading institution touched off runs on other banks. In 1933, the spark came from the difficulties of the Union Guardian Trust Co. of Detroit. On Feb 14, after its problems of frozen assets could not be solved, the State of Michigan embarked upon an eight-day holiday.

The holiday was never lifted. Depositors in other states, acquainted by newspapers and by personal experience with the havoc it began to raise, said to themselves: 'Suppose this should happen here?' The instinct of self-preservation grew increasingly stronger than reason, and the bank runs began.

City after city and state after state began to reel before the onslaught. Fear generated fear. Outwardly calm, but inwardly alarmed, depositors moved grimly on their banks. Like Norwegian lemmings, nothing stopped them . . .

When governors, after all-day and all-night meetings with legislators and bankers, proclaimed holidays and restrictions, the depositors who had not run or who were too late accepted their fate with calmness.

Across the land rolled a panorama of human reactions, now tragic, now comic, now showing amazing resourcefulness and adaptability to new and strange conditions . . .

In California, the bank holiday held up a projected hanging because it was illegal to execute anyone on a bank holiday. IOUs appeared on collection plates of churches. In a New York speakeasy, a bibulous customer asked the bartender how many states had declared bank holidays. 'Thirty-eight,' was the reply. 'Aha!' was the rejoiner. 'That ratifies the depression!'
*Newsweek*; March 11, 1933

Let me first assert my firm belief that the only thing we have to fear is fear itself—nameless, unreasoning, unjustified terror which paralyzes needed efforts to convert retreat into advance.
Franklin D. Roosevelt; Inaugural Address; March 4, 1933

Eleanor Roosevelt volunteers in soup kitchen

March 5, 1933
## 50,000 IN STREETS CHEER ROOSEVELT

I shall ask the Congress for the one remaining instrument to meet the crisis—broad Executive power to wage a war against the emergency, as great as the power that would be given me if we were invaded by a foreign foe.
ibid

## THEIR SPIRITS ARE LIFTED BY HIS SMILE OF CONFIDENCE

The people of the United States have not failed. In their need they have registered a mandate that they want direct, vigorous action. They have asked for discipline and direction under leadership. They have made me the present instrument of their wishes. In the spirit of the gift I take it.
ibid

America hasn't been as happy in three years as it is today. No money, no banks, no work, no nothing, but they know they got a man in there who is wise to Congress and wise to our so-called big men. The whole country is with him, just so he does something. Even if what he does is wrong they are with him. Just so he does something. If he burned down the Capitol, we would cheer and say, 'Well, we at least got a fire started anyhow.'
Will Rogers; March 5, 1933

Less than 34 hours after he became President of the United States, Franklin D. Roosevelt took action unprecedented in American history. By proclamation, under a war-time measure's terms, he closed the doors of every bank in the United States and its possessions . . . Essentially, the President's proclamation was an expedient to end further depression stop-gaps. Almost at one stroke it brought the banking problem to a head and centralized authority to deal with remedies. In consequence, the new administration has an unparalleled chance to bring relief more permanent than palliatives.
*Newsweek*; March 11, 1933

53

Some of our bankers had shown themselves either incompetent or dishonest in their handling of the people's funds. They had used the money entrusted to them in speculations and unwise loans. This was, of course, not true in the vast majority of our banks, but it was true in enough of them to shock the people for a time into a sense of insecurity and to put them in a frame of mind where they did not differentiate, but seemed to assume that the acts of a comparative few had tainted them all. It was the Government's job to straighten out this situation and to do it as quickly as possible. And the job is being performed . . .

Confidence and courage are the essentials in our plan. You must have faith; you must not be stampeded by rumors. We have provided the machinery to restore our financial system; it is up to you to support and make it work. Together we cannot fail.
Franklin D. Roosevelt; First Fireside Chat; March 12, 1933

Mr. Roosevelt stepped to the microphone last night and knocked another home run. His message was not only a great comfort to the people, but it pointed a lesson to all radio announcers and public speakers what to do with a big vocabulary—leave it at home in the dictionary.

Some people spend a lifetime juggling with words, with not an idea in a carload.

Our President took such a dry subject as banking (and when I say 'dry,' I mean dry, for if it had been liquid, he wouldn't have to speak on it at all) and made everybody understand it, even the bankers.
Will Rogers; March 13, 1933

March 13, 1933
## MANY BANKS IN THE CITY & NATION REOPEN TODAY FOR NORMAL OPERATIONS

Gone are my blues, and gone are my tears;
I've got good news to shout in your ears.
The silver dollar has returned to the fold,
With silver you can turn your dreams to gold.

We're in the money, we're in the money,
We've got a lot of what it takes to get along!
We're in the money, the skies are sunny;
Old man depression, you are through, you done us wrong!

We never see a headline 'bout a breadline today,
And when we see the landlord,
We can look that guy right in the eye.

We're in the money, come on my honey,
Let's spend it, lend it, send it rolling along!
**We're in the Money**; song; Warren and Dubin; 1932

President Roosevelt tossed precedent out the window at his first press conference, and inaugurated a new deal for the reporters.

Long-standing rules for the conduct of these hitherto formal sessions were shattered as the President plunged into a good-natured give-and-take with his interrogators. Quips flew back and forth, and laughter punctuated the interview. When it was over, those news-hardened recorders of tremendous events, to whom the unusual is just part of the day's work, burst into enthusiastic applause.

For the first time since the early days of the Harding Administration, the President of the United States gave direct answers to verbal questions, instead of requiring that all questions be written out and submitted in advance . . .

More than one hundred correspondents filled the room. At the outset Mr. Roosevelt said he hoped to be able to talk with complete frankness, thus making it clear that the White House 'spokesman,' that shadowy figure of the Coolidge regime, would have no place in the new Administration.
*Literary Digest*; March 25, 1933

I think this would be a good time for beer.
Franklin D. Roosevelt; March 12, 1933

### LEGAL BREW FLOODS THE COUNTRY ON WAVE OF WHOOPEE

On a vast wave of conversation, printer's ink, whooped-up hilarity, legal beer swept across the country last week.

For the time being, it surpassed the former triumphs of Mah Jong, miniature golf and Technocracy as a national theme song.

With its arrival everything else went off the front pages. Vast international happenings, war and its rumors, capitalists' attempts to conserve their system, Fascists' and Communists' attempts to overthrow it, all were swept away in the foamy flood.

City editors called on their statistical trained seals to estimate that the amount of beer sold in the United States during the first 24 hours of its appearance would float a battleship. Economists got out their pencils to figure that beer sales in the first day would result in a Federal income of from $7,500,000 to $10,000,000 from taxes

based on $5 a barrel. This based on the national delivery of from a million and a half to two million barrels . . .

New York drank its beer so fast that the supply of the 16,585 firms and individuals licensed to sell it could not keep up with the demand and for a while a shortage was threatened. Health Department license blanks under which legalized sellers were operating were not ready for the rush of New York's clamoring for 'beer papers,' so licenses were issued on blanks of the Fire Department Bureau of Combustibles.

Bostonians were so delighted with their new toy that those who swarmed into Jake Wirth's place on Stuart Street on the evening of the Great Release, would not believe the barman when the latter protested that Wirth's had not yet received its license. Reveling customers insisted on having something to drink. Underneath a large sign saying, 'This is only Near Beer—We Haven't any License Yet,' they swigged down vast quantities of near-beer while news photographers took their pictures and psychologists studied the effects of whatever it is that makes people think they are having a swell time.
*Newsweek*; April 15, 1933

**Repeal of Prohibition, 1933**

March 20, 1933
## ROOSEVELT TO BACK DIRECT CASH GRANT IN NEW RELIEF BILL
**Program Drafted Calls for $500,000,000 and for Work Camps for 500,000 Men**

March 30, 1933
## HOUSE PASSES BILL FOR FORESTRY JOBS
A new army of American pioneers will go into the woods within a few weeks. Across 150,000,000 acres of forest lands owned by the Nation and the states, an area five times as large as the state of Connecticut, will march an army of workers, now unemployed and trudging city streets.

It is estimated that under the plans of the Roosevelt Unemployment Conservation Bill, signed by the President last week, 250,000 men can shortly be put to work on reforestation. That this army will be fully enlisted by the time United States Forester R. Y. Stuart gives the command, was evident from the rain of applications that poured into Washington from all over the country.
*Newsweek*; April 8, 1933

President Franklin D. Roosevelt
The White House
Washington, D.C.                              September 9, 1933
Dear Boss,

I'll address you this way for two reasons. First you seem to be a pretty regular guy. Second you are the boss.

We have here I think one of the best [CCC] camps that could possibly be established. The country and the hills here make you think there is no such thing as a city.

I won't waste your time writing a letter about what work I have done and all I should have done.

Enclosed you will find a copy of our camp newspaper. If you like it let me know. If you don't like it make believe I didn't even send it.

Anytime you are around this part of the country, drop in and see us we are always home.

Your pal,
Bill Shand, Jr.
256-Co. C.C.C.
Blue Mt. Camp #25
Peekskill, N.Y.

It sure beats 'Brother, can you spare a dime?'
CCC boy after two weeks in camp

April 20, 1933
## U.S. OFF GOLD STANDARD, ROOSEVELT TO RULE CURRENCY; STOCKS AND COMMODITIES SOAR

[The papers] say we are off the gold. The best way to tell when each of us went off the gold is to figure back how many years it was since we had any . . . The last I remember getting my clutches on was in Johannesburg, South Africa, some five dollars in English gold pieces that we carried in a belt around our waist. I used the last one to pay a third class passage to Australia, so I went off gold in 1902. So this move strikes me as no great novelty or calamity.
Will Rogers; April 23, 1933

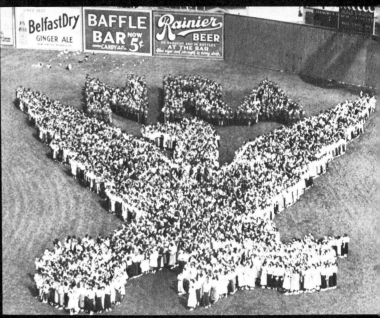

Below: Civilian Conservation Corps boys in camp

May 12, 1933
## INDUSTRY CONTROL BILL READY TODAY

May 12, 1933
## 25,000 JOBS OPENED TO BONUS SEEKERS; ROOSEVELT OFFERS CAMP WORK AS MORE MARCHERS ARRIVE IN WASHINGTON

In an unexpected move providing a direct answer to the thousands of World War veterans marching into Washington to reassert their demand for immediate cash payment of the bonus, President Roosevelt today offered jobs in the emergency conservation corps for 25,000 bonafide ex-servicemen.
*New York Herald Tribune*

May 13, 1933
## PRESIDENT SIGNS FARM BILL; ASKS FORECLOSURE DELAY

June 14, 1933
## ROOSEVELT SIGNS RELIEF BILL FOR HOME OWNERS
### Asks Halt on Foreclosure Until Machinery Is Set Up for Refinancing Mortgages

June 17, 1933
## BILL TO PROTECT BANK DEPOSITS BECOMES LAW

A reporter made Franklin D. Roosevelt chuckle with a story of an old lady in Chicago who complained that she spent all of her small change buying hourly editions of afternoon papers to learn what the President had done since the last edition.
*Newsweek*; 1933

June 17, 1933
## ROOSEVELT OPENS RECOVERY DRIVE; 5 MILLION NEW JOBS HIS GOAL; PUBLIC ASKED TO SUPPORT PROGRAM

If all employers in each competitive group agree to pay their workers the same wages—reasonable wages—and require the same hours—reasonable hours—then higher wages and shorter hours will hurt no employer. Moreover, such action is better for the employer than unemployment and low wages, because it makes more buyers for his product. That is the simple idea which is the very heart of the Industrial Recovery Act [NRA].

On the basis of this simple principle of everybody doing things together, we are starting out on this nation-wide attack on unemployment. It will succeed if our people understand it—in the big industries, in the little shops, in the great cities and in the small villages. There is nothing complicated about it and there is nothing particularly new in the principle. It goes back to the basic idea of society and of the nation itself that people acting in a group can accomplish things which no individual acting alone could even hope to bring about . . .

There are, of course, men, a few of them who might thwart this great common purpose by seeking selfish advantage. There are adequate penalties in the law, but I am now asking the cooperation that comes from opinion and from conscience. These are the only

MEMBER
NRA
U.S.
WE DO OUR PART

instruments we shall use in this great summer offensive against unemployment. But we shall use them to the limit to protect the willing from the laggard and to make the plan succeed.

In war, in the gloom of night attack, soldiers wear a bright badge on their shoulders to be sure that comrades do not fire on comrades. On that principle, those who cooperate in this program must know each other at a glance. That is why we have provided a badge of honor for this purpose, a simple design with a legend, 'We do our part,' and I ask that all those who join with me shall display that badge prominently. It is essential to our purpose.

Franklin D. Roosevelt; Fireside Chat; July 24, 1933

Nothing can stop the President's program, nothing will even hamper the President's program . . . The power of this people, once aroused and united in a fixed purpose, is the most irresistible force in the world.

Of course, there are ways to beat the rules of any game. We know what they are. We are not issuing any regulations about that. We are just asking people in this crisis, in very general terms, to rise above these cheap little ingenuities and to join with the President to beat the depression and not to beat the rules of the game.

General Hugh S. Johnson; NRA Administrator; July, 1933

Why is everybody gazing up in the air, with a smile on their face?
Just hear them sing. Everybody's happy, not a one has a care;
Why they've got me doing the same darn thing!

There is a New Eagle, up in the sky,
The Blue Eagle, he's flying high,
This mammoth bird is soaring near and far,
He brings a cheerful word from FDR.
In his mighty claws, he holds a mighty cause;
A brand new understanding,
We know he'll make a happy landing;
Blue Eagle, he'll do or die, the Blue Eagle's flying high!

**The Blue Eagle's Flying High**; song; Baskette and Alban; 1933

This is Chapter 1—in epitome—of the Roosevelt regime. And what a chapter! What a regime! . . .

Fifteen weeks of high-pressure activity. Fifteen weeks of whirlwind changes in the old order, of experimental panaceas, of legislative novelties and of practically unchallenged Executive domination of the colossal organism which we call the Federal Government.

More history has been made during these fifteen weeks than in any comparable peacetime period since Americans went into business for themselves on this continent. The legislation that has now been written into law, under the Roosevelt leadership, touches some of them lightly and by indirection only. It touches others heavily and will leave a mark on them not to be erased for a generation, if at all.

Powers have been reposed in the Presidency that have made that office a virtual dictatorship. It may be looked upon both as a benevolent and a necessary dictatorship. Undoubtedly it is so looked upon in most quarters. It may not be irrevocable. But soften the phrasing as much as one may, the fact remains that the present governmental set-up amounts to temporary Executive absolutism.

*Literary Digest*; July, 1933

# DON'T SHOOT, G-MEN, DON'T SHOOT!

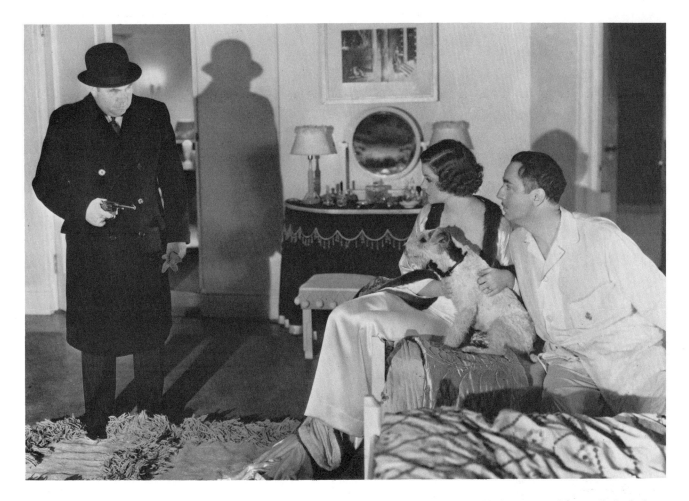

## Noon Street Nemesis

Pete Anglich looked after the Duesenberg. It was opposite the row of billboards that screened the parking lot. It was barely crawling now. Something sailed from its left front window, fell with a dry slap on the sidewalk. The car picked up speed soundlessly, purred off into the darkness. A block away its head lights flashed up full again.

Nothing moved. The thing that had been thrown out of the car lay on the inner edge of the sidewalk, almost under one of the billboards.

Then the girl was coming back again, a step at a time, haltingly. Pete Anglich watched her come, without moving. When she was level with him he said softly: 'What's the racket? Could a fellow help?'

She spun around with a choked sound, as though she had forgotten all about him. Her head moved in the darkness at his side. There was a swift shine as her eyes moved. There was a pale flicker across her chin. Her voice was low, hurried, scared.

'You're the man from the lunch wagon. I saw you.'

'Open up. What is it—a pay-off?'

Her head moved again in the darkness at his side, up and down.

'What's in the package?' Pete Anglich growled. 'Money?'

Her words came in a rush. 'Would you get it for me? Oh, would you please? I'd be so grateful. I'd—'

He laughed. His laugh had a low growling sound. 'Get it for *you*, baby? I use money in my business, too. Come on, what's the racket? Spill.'

She jerked away from him, but he didn't let go of her arm. He slid the gun out of sight under his coat, held her with both hands. Her voice sobbed as she whispered: 'He'll kill me, if I don't get it.'

Walter Long, Myrna Loy and William Powell in *The Thin Man*, 1934

Very sharply, coldly, Pete Anglich said, 'Who will?' . . .

His voice was hard, angry. 'Oh, hell, stay here and I'll get your damn pay-off for you.'

He left the girl and went lightly along close to the front of the apartment house. At the edge of the billboards he stopped, probed the darkness with his eyes, saw the package. It was wrapped in dark material, not large but large enough to see. He bent down and looked under the billboards. He didn't see anything behind them.

He went on four steps, leaned down and picked up the package, felt cloth and two thick rubber bands. He stood quite still, listening.

Distant traffic hummed on a main street. A light burned across the street in a rooming house, behind a glass-paneled door. A window was open and dark above it.

A woman's voice screamed shrilly behind him.

He stiffened, whirled, and the light hit him between the eyes. It came from the dark window across the street, a blinding white shaft that impaled him against the billboard.

His face leered in it, his eyes blinked. He didn't move any more.

Shoes dropped on cement and a smaller spot stabbed at him sideways from the end of the billboards. Behind the spot a casual voice spoke: 'Don't shift an eyelash, bud. You're all wrapped up in law.'

**Noon Street Nemesis**; Raymond Chandler;
*Detective Fiction Weekly*; May 30, 1936


If you want to understand the criminal brain, you must become a momentary actor. For the time, dispel all your thoughts of responsibility. You owe nothing to anyone but yourself. You must have no sense of loyalty, even to your best friends, but be willing to throw them to the wolves the moment their interests interfere with yours. Become selfish to the degree that anyone who blocks you in your desires is an enemy to be dealt with as foully as you feel he is dealing with you. Remember that what you want you must have, no matter how you get it . . . School yourself to think that you amount to something if you can get away with murder, and that you really have achieved a great niche in life, if, with several companions armed with machine guns, you have held up and robbed a bank . . .

View any and all means, whether they be stealth, lies, forgery, perjury, the bribery of witnesses, intimidation, the pleading of reform, evidences of remorse, eagerness for rehabilitation, or the feigning of illness and even the death of your own mother, as right and proper if used by you to escape a sentence for your deeds, or to persuade guileless persons to aid you in leaving a prison cell. Consider any part of the world which runs contrariwise to your narrow, cheap, selfish, egoistic nature as being 'against you.' Look upon wealth gained from honest effort as luck, and consider everybody lucky but yourself, thereby entitling you to 'make your own luck.' Be maudlin concerning yourself and cynical about the feelings of others. Believe yourself fine and noble if you indulge in cheap sentimentalities about sweethearts, parents, babies or animals, thus building a psychology by which you can condone murder if 'you have always been a good boy to your mother.' However, should these components become impedimental, have no compunction whatever about deserting your sweetheart, using your mother's home as a hideout, shooting down a baby or choking your dog, all to the purpose that you hate to do it, but after all, you've got to live. To believe all these things implicitly is to have the true criminal viewpoint.

**Persons in Hiding**; J. Edgar Hoover; 1938

Al Capone

They call Capone a bootlegger. Yes. It's bootleg while it's on the trucks, but when your host at the club, in the locker room or on the Gold Coast hands it to you on a silver platter, it's hospitality. What's Al done, then? He's supplied a legitimate demand. Some call it bootlegging. Some call it racketeering. I call it business. They say I violate the prohibition law. Who doesn't?
Al Capone; 1930

June 6, 1931
## CAPONE GIVES UP TO U.S.; INDICTED ON INCOME TAX

June 13, 1931
## INDICT CAPONE & 68 IN BEER CONSPIRACY;
### Federal Agents Make 5,000 Charges
### Against Gang Leader & his Henchmen

'Go out and actually prove that Al Capone is at the head of this liquor conspiracy,' this special group of . . . six [Federal] prohibition enforcement men, headed by Assistant Chief Special Agent Eliot Ness . . . was ordered. So its members, most of them carrying on other regular duties, proceeded quietly to remove the aura of immunity that had been placed upon the dark brow of 'Scarface Al' Capone by his gangland followers.

It wasn't long before Chicago's hoodlum world became aware of the persistently annoying activity of the seven men. They began to be known among the gangsters by extremely undignified and unprintable names.

But Agent Ness, now 28 years old—six years removed from his commencement day at the University of Chicago—had studied history during his college days. He is also possessed of a sense of humor. He remembered that the appellations employed to describe his group had been used in the caste history of India to describe the 'untouchables.'

So 'untouchables' it was. And now that word has come to designate the kind of modern government agent, grown up out of prohibition enforcement, who cannot be 'touched' by the bribes of gangsters and liquor syndicates.
*New York Times*; June 18, 1931

I've been made an issue, I guess, and I'm not complaining. But why don't they go after all these bankers who took the savings of thousands of poor people and lost them in the failures? How about that?

Isn't it lots worse to take the last few dollars some small family has saved—perhaps to live on while the head of the family is out of a job —than to sell a little beer, a little alky?

Believe me, I can't see where the fellow who sells it is any worse off than the fellow who buys it and drinks it.
Al Capone; July, 1931

June 17, 1931
## CAPONE PLEADS GUILTY TO THREE INDICTMENTS

. . . A year ago the average Chicagoan would have laughed had he heard a prediction of that court-room scene of defeat for Scarface. Orderly citizens and racketeers alike would have laughed. For Capone was immune. Did he not have millions at his disposal? Had he not 'bought' public officials? Had he not 'greased' his way wherever he wanted to go in Chicago? Was he not the most powerful racketeer of all time? The impossible had happened.
*New York Times*; June 21, 1931

July 31, 1931
## CAPONE CHANGES PLEA TO NOT GUILTY

What the well-dressed gangster wears, including a $135 custom-made suit and $275 diamond belt buckle, was brought out in full detail today at Scarface Al Capone's trial on income tax evasion charges . . .

Capone, biggest gangster of them all, was said by the (department store) clerks ordinarily to wear about $700 worth of fine raiment. His customary dress included a $27.50 shirt with $1 monogram; $4.95 tie; $2 collar; $135 suit; $150 overcoat; $275 belt buckle; $10 suit of silk underwear; $20 hat; $20 shoes and $2 socks.

Because he usually was busy with pressing affairs—which the prosecutors charged were gambling, liquor and vice—Capone bought his fine quality suits by the half dozens and his expensive shirts in even larger numbers, the clerks said . . .

The defendant's appearance in court seemed to uphold the department store clerks' testimony—today he wore a new green hat, a grayish overcoat with brown velvet collar, dark gray suit, bright yellow shoes and a diamond-flecked watch chain extended across his portly vest.

*New York Daily News*; October 13, 1931

Gangsters and racketeers play so prominent a part in the American life of today that it would be little short of a miracle if their exploits were ignored by the movies. Nor are they. In fact, the number of films dealing with the underworld and its criminal activities is altogether too great . . . The week under review saw four new pictures in New York belonging to this class . . .

It is the business of movies, as it is of the theatre, to reflect life, and American life is American life. The trouble with these films is that they reflect the life of the underworld in a light that is altogether false. They crown the hold-up man and the safe-breaker with the romantic halo of bravery and adventure that helps to disguise their fundamental moronism. Nor do they ever make the slightest attempt to relate the criminal class to its social source, the economics and spirit of rapacious capitalism.

**The Underworld**; Alexander Bashky; *Nation*; January 21, 1931

You know, these gang pictures—that's terrible kid stuff. Why, they ought to take all of them and throw them in the lake. They're doing nothing but harm the younger element of this country. I don't blame the censors for trying to bar them.

Al Capone; July 30, 1931

October 18, 1931
## CAPONE FOUND GUILTY

I guess a guy can't try to do the right thing without getting in a mess.
Al Capone; October 18, 1931

October 25, 1931
## CAPONE GETS 11 YEARS

Well, I'm on my way to do eleven years. I've got to do it that's all. I'm not sore at anybody. Some people are lucky. I wasn't.

There was too much overhead in my business anyhow, paying off all the time and replacing trucks and breweries. They ought to make it legitimate.

Al Capone to Elliot Ness; November, 1931

March 2, 1932

**LINDBERGH BABY KIDNAPPED FROM HIS HOME AT NIGHT**

The most famous baby in the world, Charles A. Lindbergh, Jr., was kidnapped from his crib on the second floor of the Lone Eagle's estate in the woods at Hopewell, New Jersey, between 7:30 and 10:30 last night . . .

Colonel Charles A. Lindbergh called Major Charles F. Schoeffel, State Superintendant of Police, and within an hour the largest hunt for kidnappers in the history of the nation was underway.
*New York Daily News*

March 3, 1932

From President Hoover to the youngest policeman on the beat, the whole machinery of the nation was in full operation with sympathy and indignation spurring men and women to extraordinary efforts on behalf of the missing child.
*New York Herald Tribune*

It's the most outrageous thing I have ever heard of . . . I'll give $10,000 for information that will lead to recovery of the child unharmed, and the capture of his kidnappers.

If I were out of jail I could be of real assistance. I have friends all over the country who could aid in running this thing down.
Al Capone; March, 1932

March 3, 1932

[In] the greatest concentration of Federal forces upon a single crime in many years, a disturbed Congress whipped into shape bills carrying drastic penalties for kidnapping. While denunciation of the crime and sympathy for Colonel and Mrs. Charles A. Lindbergh were feelingly expressed on the floors of the Senate and House, the Judiciary Committees of both houses prepared to act on a bill imposing the death penalty at the discretion of the Federal courts for the transportation of kidnapped persons across state lines.

*New York Herald Tribune*

May 13, 1932

## GET THE LINDBERGH KILLERS!

The kidnapped Lindbergh baby has been found—slain.

The damnable fiends, the inhuman monsters, who kidnapped the baby and presumably were responsible for the bilking of Colonel Lindbergh out of $50,000 are still at large.

Until the killers are tracked down and brought to justice, the children of America will not be safe. And the rest of the world will be able to point to this country and say: 'That is the country where criminals can persecute decent citizens in absolute defiance of the law.'

*New York Daily News*

I have directed the law enforcement agencies and the several Secret Services of the Federal Government to make the kidnapping and murder of the Lindbergh baby a live and never-to-be-forgotten case until the criminals are implacably brought to justice.

Herbert Hoover; May 14, 1932

The man reached into the watch pocket of his trousers and extracted a bill. He tossed it through the opening of the ticket booth. 'One in the orchestra,' he said.

The bill was folded once lengthwise, and twice crosswise, making a small oblong of little more than an inch each way. Miss Barr [the ticket cashier] unfolded the note and began to examine it to ascertain whether it was genuine. She had detected many counterfeits in her time.

The bill was a five-dollar Federal Reserve note. It bore a yellow seal. As Miss Barr fingered the bill, the man asked; 'What's the matter, it's gut, ain't it?' His gaze was level, his voice devoid of feeling, coated with a thick German accent. Miss Barr hung on to that word 'gut.'

'It's a perfectly good bill,' answered the cashier. 'Only it is a Federal Reserve gold note and should have been turned into the Government.' . . .

The teller walked hurriedly to the desk of one of the bank's officers, and placed the bill on the officer's desk.

'Here's one of the Lindbergh ransom bills, sir,' he said. 'I have just checked it. It came in with the Sheridan Theatre deposit last night.'

*True Detective*: January, 1935

September 21, 1934

## LINDBERGH RANSOM RECEIVER SEIZED, $13,750 FOUND
### Kidnap Suspect Was Carpenter Near Baby's Home
### 2½-Year Hunt For Murderer Seen Near End

The Lindbergh kidnapping case, one of the most sensational crimes in the nation's history, was near solution last night, police and Federal authorities announced, following the arrest of a Bronx carpenter . . .

The prisoner is Bruno Richard Hauptmann, 35 years old, living with his wife and ten-month-old son at 1279 East 222nd Street, in the Wakefield section of the Bronx. A German convict out on parole, he entered this country illegally as a stowaway eleven years ago.
*New York Herald Tribune*

January 2, 1935
## HAUPTMANN TRIAL WILL START TODAY
**Flemington [New Jersey] Thronged
on Eve of Hearing for Man Accused
of Killing Lindbergh Baby**

[Newspaper] circulation, as everybody knows, has been bad the last few months. There is more human interest in the Lindbergh case than in any other world event. The attempt to translate this human interest into circulation figures has made of Flemington a frenzied community with but a single thought. There are 700 newspapermen in town, including 129 camera men. Two hundred newspapers have their own correspondents on the scene. Hearst heads the list with fifty representatives, including, appropriately enough, his star sports writer and his Hollywood expert. The New York World-Telegram has eleven men on the case, the Philadelphia Bulletin nine. The population of Flemington, normally 2,800, has been augmented by some 1,200.
**The Biggest Show on Earth**; Margaret Marshall; *Nation*; January 23, 1935

February 14, 1935
## HAUPTMANN GUILTY—MUST DIE

The dispassionate historian will now concede that the trial of Richard Bruno Hauptmann was not the most important historical event of the last thousand years. It will generally be admitted that the invention of printing, the discovery of America, and the World War have had greater earth-shaking consequences. Even certain contemporary occurrences may come to be regarded as having more vitally affected the lives and happiness of mankind.

It is well to bear this in mind. For with the clamor and ballyhoo of the exhibition at Flemington still echoing in our ears, with the bewildering journalistic orgy still fresh in our minds, with a recent recollection of the absurdities and vulgarities of the case, it is difficult to realize that what we have been witnessing was a demonstration of American criminal justice in action . . .

It is not disputed, of course, that this was an intrinsically great case. It had all the ingredients that a master of detective fiction would think of in his most inspired moments. The principal victims was one of the most famous characters in the world; the crime was surrounded by baffling mystery, shot through with cross currents of romance, intrigue and suicide; the detective work, implemented by the most advanced discoveries of modern science, surpassed in brilliancy the greatest achievements of Sherlock Holmes. Even the world economic crisis, which resulted in the United States going off the gold standard, conspired to track down the murderer. And finally, that supreme element in all great mysteries, a lingering doubt that still persists in the minds of many as to the extent of the convicted defendant's actual complicity.
**Justice Goes Tabloid**; Newman Levy; *American Mercury*; April, 1935

April 4, 1936
**BRUNO DIES IN CHAIR; LIPS LOCKED TO END**

J. Edgar Hoover observes FBI
target practice

Kidnappers get at least one person every twenty-four hours. The homes of the rich are today homes of fear. Even those with moderate savings are apprehensive. Citizens by the hundreds are sending to the Division of Investigation of the United States Department of Justice in Washington for noncriminal fingerprint cards, that their fingerprints may be on file for identification purposes if they should suddenly disappear . . .

The bulky man who paces in front of the house is an armed guard. The nurse who takes the children to school is often an armed female detective. And in many schools teachers are required to see that their wards are safely started homewards, free from a call into some stranger's automobile. Such is the fear of the Snatch Racket.
**Closing in on the Kidnappers**; *American Magazine*; May, 1934

July 24, 1933
### TWO MACHINE GUN KIDNAPPERS GET RICH OIL MAN
Oklahoma City—Police and Federal authorities united today in a widespread search for Charles F. Urschel, wealthy oil operator, and two men who kidnapped him in a daring raid on his home late last night.

Bearing machine guns, the two broke in upon a sun porch bridge game in which Mr. and Mrs. Urschel and Walter R. Jarrett, a neighboring oil man, and his wife, participated . . .

Jarrett said he believed the gunmen were 'professionals,' were acquainted with Oklahoma City streets and hoped to leave the impression that Charles 'Pretty Boy' Floyd, notorious desperado, was involved.
*New York Herald Tribune*

January 19, 1934

**KIDNAPPERS HOLD ST. PAUL BANKER FOR $200,000**

St. Paul, Minnesota—While picked Federal agents swooped in airplanes to this city for a new war on brazen kidnappers, the family of Edward G. Bremer, banker and son of a close friend of President Roosevelt, opened negotiations tonight with the gang who seized him yesterday morning after he had driven his daughter, Betty, 7, to school.

*New York Daily News*

A telephone rings late at night in the Department of Justice Building in Washington. A husky, curly-haired man, who looks something like Admiral Byrd, lifts the receiver. From a Middle-Western town comes the hysterical voice of a woman whose husband has been kidnapped. The man takes notes as he listens.

'We'll get busy right away, madam,' he says.

He picks up another telephone and makes two long-distance calls, quietly despatching his nearest agents to the scene. Before they can climb into their fast cars he has moved two pins, which represent men on his big wall map, into their new position. J. Edgar Hoover, director of the department's Division of Investigation, has another case.

*Newsweek*; August 12, 1933

I stand squarely behind the efforts of the Department of Justice to bring to book every law breaker, big and little.

Franklin D. Roosevelt; May 19, 1934

From the top: Ma Barker, Fred Barker, Pretty Boy Floyd, Machine Gun Kelly. Opposite: John Dillinger with wooden pistol used in the Lake County Jail break, March 1934

September 27, 1933

## KIDNAPPING KELLY FALLS IN U.S. TRAP

Memphis, Tenn—George E. (Machine Gun) Kelly, notorious desperado, surrendered without a struggle here today as a detective sergeant pointed a sawed-off shotgun at his heart. The Southwest's bad man was asleep in a bungalow this morning when Department of Justice agents quietly perfected arrangements for his capture to face trial in the $200,000 kidnapping of Charles F. Urschel, Oklahoma City oil man.

The house in which Kelly and his red-haired wife, Kathryn, and two others were staying, was surrounded by police. Officer Bill Raney entered a front door. As Kelly opened a bedroom door, revolver in hand, Raney told him quietly:

'Drop that gun, Kelly.'

'Don't shoot, G-men; don't shoot!' Kelly's pistol dropped to the floor. His hands pointed to the ceiling.

*New York Daily News*

January 17, 1935

## TWO BREMER KIDNAPPERS SLAIN; FRED BARKER AND 'MA' DIE;

### Shoot to the Last When Trapped By Federal Agents in Florida; Weapons Blaze for Six Hours in Oklahoma as Prostrate Villagers Look On

Federal agents trailed 'Ma' Barker and her son, Fred, long sought as members of the gang that kidnapped Edward G. Bremer, St. Paul banker, to their Florida hiding place today and killed them both after a machine gun battle lasting six hours.

Mrs. Kate (Ma) Barker who has been called the brains of the Barker-Karpis gang held responsible for the kidnapping of Mr. Bremer died with a machine gun in her hand. Residents of this little village described the scene as 'like a war'.

*New York Times*

If I seem to be vindictive toward the extortioner, it is because I regard him as the cheapest and most rodentlike of the viler criminals. Of the hundreds of cases which have come to my observation in the last few years, there has not been one in which the culprit displayed even the questionable ethics of a first-class sneak thief.

**Persons in Hiding**; J. Edgar Hoover

July 18, 1933

## DALESVILLE BANK ROBBED OF $3,500

I'm John Dillinger's father and . . . I don't think he's done near as much as they claim he has.

Dillinger's crime record since his parole from Indiana State Prison on May 23, 1933:

**July 17** Dalesville, Indiana Commercial Bank robbed of $3,500. Dillinger suspected.

**August 5** Montpelier, Indiana National Bank robbed of $12,000. Dillinger suspected.

**September 22** Dillinger arrested in Dayton, Ohio. Identified by victims as participant in bank robberies at New Carlisle, Ohio; Farrel, Pa; Indianapolis and Bluffton, Ohio. Total of $82,800 taken in these robberies.

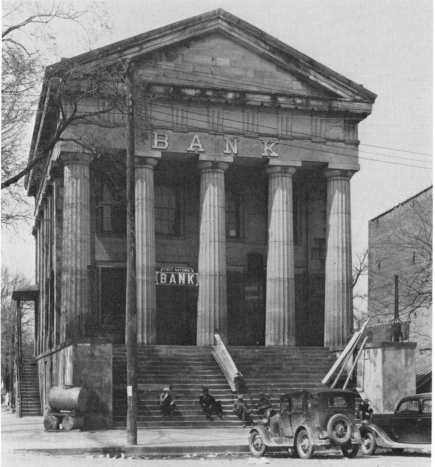

I smoke very little and I don't drink much. I guess my only bad habit is robbing banks.
John Dillinger; 1934

**September 28** Dillinger turned over to Sheriff Jess Sarber, of Allen County, Ohio at Lima for the $2,800 Bluffton bank hold-up.
**October 21** Dillinger released from the Lima jail by three confederates, who shot and killed Sheriff Sarber when he resisted the jail delivery.

His lawyer says the desperado has claustrophobia, a dread of confined spaces. Therefore he does not like staying in jails.
*Newsweek*; March 10, 1934

**November 14** Dillinger eludes trap set for him by Chicago police and Indiana officers at dentist's office.
**November 20** Racine, Wisconsin American Bank & Trust Co. robbed of $27,000 by five machine-gunners. Dillinger named by victims as leader.
**January 14** East Chicago, Indiana bank robbed of $15,000 and Policeman William P. O'Malley slain by the bandits. Dillinger identified as leader of the gang.
**January 25** Dillinger, Charles Makley, and Russell Clark, former prison companions in Indiana, with women companions, arrested in Tucson, Arizona by police there after a fireman who had been tipped generously by Dillinger for saving personal belongings in a fire, recognized the criminal's photograph in a detective magazine.

# WANTED

# JOHN HERBERT DILLINGER

On June 23, 1934, HOMER S. CUMMINGS, Attorney General of the United States, under the authority vested in him by an Act of Congress approved June 6, 1934, offered a reward of

# $10,000.00

for the capture of John Herbert Dillinger or a reward of

# $5,000.00

for information leading to the arrest of John Herbert Dillinger.

## DESCRIPTION

Age, 32 years; Height, 5 feet 7-1/8 inches; Weight, 153 pounds; Build, medium; Hair, medium chestnut; Eyes, grey; Complexion, medium; Occupation, machinist; Marks and scars, 1/2 inch scar back left hand, scar middle upper lip, brown mole between eyebrows.

All claims to any of the aforesaid rewards and all questions and disputes that may arise as among claimants to the foregoing rewards shall be passed upon by the Attorney General and his decisions shall be final and conclusive. The right is reserved to divide and allocate portions of any of said rewards as between several claimants. No part of the aforesaid rewards shall be paid to any official or employee of the Department of Justice.

If you are in possession of any information concerning the whereabouts of John Herbert Dillinger, communicate immediately by telephone or telegraph collect to the nearest office of the Division of Investigation, United States Department of Justice, the local addresses of which are set forth on the reverse side of this notice.

JOHN EDGAR HOOVER, DIRECTOR,
DIVISION OF INVESTIGATION,
UNITED STATES DEPARTMENT OF JUSTICE,
WASHINGTON, D.C.

June 25, 1934

We're exactly like you cops. You have a profession—we have a profession. Only difference is you're on the right side of the law, we're on the wrong.
John Dillinger to Tucson Police; January, 1934

**January 30** Dillinger returned by airplane to Indiana authorities at Crown Point for O'Malley slaying.

I'm for Roosevelt all the way, and for the NRA—particularly for banks.
John Dillinger at Crown Point Jail; January, 1934

**March 3** Dillinger escaped from Crown Point jail.

March 4, 1934
In a matchless piece of bravado—which eventually assumed both the proportions and the atmosphere of a comic opera—Dillinger escaped from the 'escape-proof' Lake County Jail this morning, after intimidating thirty-three jailers and inmates, with a wooden pistol, and locking them in their living quarters, closets and cells.
  With a colored confederate, also held for murder, he then seized two sub-machine guns from the warden's office of the jail, scaled a wall, commandeered the private car of Lake County's woman sheriff, and rode past a cordon of fifty guards who had been stationed around the prison especially to keep him safely inside.
*New York Sunday News*

Pulling that off was worth ten years of my life. Ha! Ha!
John Dillinger in letter to sister; March, 1934

**March 31** Dillinger and man and woman companions shot way out of police trap in St. Paul, Minnesota; trail of blood believed to indicate Dillinger wounded.

John Dillinger (if it was he) and his confederate, John Hamilton (if he has not been dead for six months), escaped Saturday from a police trap in St. Paul, Minn. Earlier in the week they had been seen in San Bernadino, Calif., and Detroit, Mich., on the same day . . .
  Meanwhile Chicago chuckled over a story of two automobiles, one from Indiana and one with Illinois plates which spent hours chasing each other around the Windy City. When at last they met, out of each car bounded police, mutually convinced that the other machine contained Dillinger.
*Newsweek*; April 3, 1934

**April 8** Dillinger visited relatives at home town of Mooresville, Indiana.
**April 12** Dillinger, with another machine-gunner Homer Van Meter, raided police station at Warsaw, Indiana and stole four bullet-proof vests and two revolvers after beating Patrolman Jud Pittenger.
**April 13** Dillinger seen by thirty men in Brownsburg, Indiana where he stopped for a hair cut, a meal and gasoline.
**April 22** Dillinger escaped trap by Federal agents at Manitowish, Wisconsin, two killed and four wounded.

April 23, 1934

J. Edgar Hoover, chief of the Department of Justice bureau of identification, announced at 2:30 o'clock this morning that John Dillinger, notorious Indiana desperado and fugitive, had been surrounded in the forests close by Mercer, Wisconsin.

However, in contradiction to this announcement came a story that three unoffending citizens, apparently mistaken for Dillinger and companions, had been fired on by Federal agents. One of these men was killed. The two others were wounded.

*New York Daily News*

Well they had Dillinger surrounded and was all ready to shoot him when he come out, but another bunch of folks come out ahead, so they just shot them instead. Dillinger is going to accidentally get with some innocent bystanders some time, then he will get shot.'

Will Rogers; April, 1934

**April 23** Three of Dillinger's gang exchanged shots with police in suburb of St. Paul; one believed wounded; gang stole auto from motorist and disappeared.

**May 1** Dillinger recognized and pursued by Chicago policeman who the desperado hit over head with pistol.

Henry Ford
Ford Motor Co., Detroit, Mich.

Hello Old Pal:

Arrived here at 10 AM today. Would like to drop in and see you.

You have a wonderful car. Been driving it for three weeks. It's a treat to drive one.

Your slogan should be:

Drive a Ford and watch the other cars fall behind you. I can make any other car take a Ford's dust.

Bye-Bye
John Dillinger

**June 28** Dillinger's father disclosed that he had received a letter from his son postmarked Chicago stating that John was alright.
**June 30** Dillinger believed by police in South Bend, Indiana to have looted a bank there of $28,439.

An innkeeper in the sleepy English city of Stratford-on-Avon hears four Rhodes scholars talking 'deucedly tough' American slang, calls the police and has them arrested, convinced that they are members of the Dillinger gang . . .

. . . Uncanny powers are apparently ascribed to him. He is supposed not only to be able to appear and disappear at will, but even to appear in several places simultaneously. One day he is said to be in Indiana, the next day in London. One day he is discovered in Michigan, the next day on the high seas. One day he is reported alive, the next dead.
*Literary Digest*; June 30, 1934

July 24, 1934
## DILLINGER SHOT TO DEATH BY FEDERAL AGENTS AS HE LEAVES CHICAGO THEATER
John Dillinger, arch criminal of the age, was shot dead tonight by a group of Department of Justice operatives as he walked out of a Chicago theater.

He whipped an automatic revolver out of his pocket and had it half raised when the operatives loosed a withering blast of revolver fire that dropped him mortally wounded. He died a few minutes later.
*New York Herald Tribune*

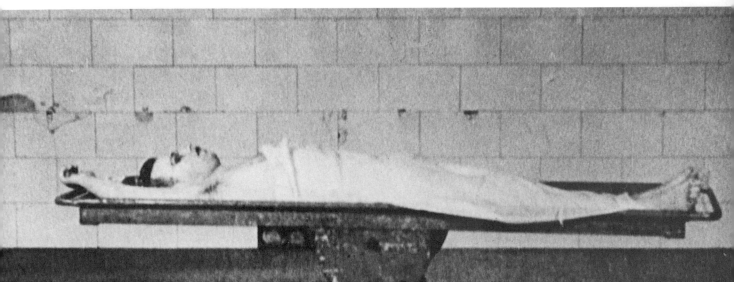

I'm awful sorry John got into this trouble and sorry that it ended up the way it has . . . I want the people to know that I tried to bring him up right and he's always been a good-hearted boy.
John Dillinger's father, July 1934

# THE DYING LAND

Southwest is parched. Temperature above 100 in shade for forty-three successive days. Missouri Pacific Railway hauling tankcars of water for use of livestock. First time in history. Sam Nance, farmer near Ardmore, Oklahoma, shoots 143 head of cattle to save them from starving. Cotton crop one-half normal. Apples, peaches, small fruits 30 percent normal. Livestock congesting packing centers. Beef selling on foot as low as $.01 a pound. Pasturage exhausted. States too broke to grant drought aid. United States adjudges 81 counties for primary emergency relief; 119 for secondary. Arkansas river four feet below normal record. Town and city reservoirs failing. Churches praying for rain in many parts of Arkansas, Oklahoma and Texas.

**Saga of Drought**; Charles Morrow Wilson; *Commonweal*; September 14, 1934

February 24, 1935
## NEW DUST STORM SWEEPS THE PLAINS

February 26, 1935
## BLIZZARD OF SLEET AND HAIL FOLLOWS TORNADOES AND DUST; HEAVY CROP LOSSES REPORTED IN MANY STATES

March 6, 1935
## DUST STORM FROM WEST GIVES KANSAS A BLUE SUN

The cloud extended east and west as far as could be seen in a straight line. As it came on it presented a rolling, tumbling appearance, something like a great wall of muddy water.

The base was inky black, the top portion of a lighter color.

Hundreds of geese and ducks and smaller birds too numerous to count were racing for their lives . . . The almost entire absence of all birds following the storm was one proof of its severity.

A. A. Justice, meteorologist, describing Dodge City, Kansas dust storm; April, 1935

The impact is like a shovelful of fine sand flung against the face. People caught in their own yards grope for the doorstep. Cars come to a standstill, for no light in the world can penetrate that swirling murk.

Dust masks are snatched from pockets and cupboards. But masks do not protect the mouth. Grit cracks between the teeth, the dust taste lies bitter on the tongue, grime is harsh between the lips.

The house rocks and mumbles . . . The family huddles together. If quiet storms excite brooding anxiety, this one is pure terror even to plains people hardened to the wind. The darkness is like the end of the world.

In time the fury subsides. If the wind has spent itself, the dust will fall silently for hours. If the wind has settled into a good steady blow, the air will be thick for days. During those days as much of living as possible will be moved to the basement, while pounds and pounds of dust sift into the house. It is something, however, to have the house stop rocking and mumbling.

The nightmare is deepest during the storms. But on the occasional bright day and the usual gray day we cannot shake free from it. We live with the dust, eat it, sleep with it, watch it strip us of possessions and the hope of possessions. It is becoming the Real. The poetic uplift of spring fades into a phantom of the storied past.

The nightmare is becoming Life.

**Dust**; Avis D. Carlson; *New Republic*; May 1, 1935

Long about Nineteen thirty-one,
My field burnt up in the boiling sun.
Long about Nineteen thirty-two,
Dust did rise and the dust it blew.
End o' my line, end o' my line,
I reckon I come to the end o' my line.
Long about Nineteen thirty-three,
Living in the dust was a-killing me.
Long about Nineteen thirty-four,
Dangburn dust it blew some more.
Long about Nineteen thirty-five,
Blowed my crops about nine miles high.
End o' my line, end o' my line,
I reckon I come to the end o' my line.
**End o' my Line**; song; Woody Guthrie

There is a current story in southwest Kansas about a man who, hit on the head by a raindrop, was so overcome that two buckets of sand had to be thrown in his face to revive him . . . The plain folk, they say, have adopted a new device to show not only the direction of the wind but the force. It consists of a tall pole, with a steel logging chain attached to it. If the chain blows out horizontally it's only a breeze; if the links at the end of the chain begin to snap you call it a wind. If the whole chain flies to pieces and the pole blows over it is a Kansas Twister.

**Kansas Grit**; Josephine Strode; *Survey*; August, 1936

Eva, Oklahoma
June 30, 1935

My dear Evelyn:

In the dust-covered desolation of our No Man's Land here, wearing our shade hats, with handkerchiefs tied over our faces, and vaseline in our nostrils, we have been trying to rescue our home from the wind-blown dust which penetrates wherever air can go. It is almost a hopeless task, for there is rarely a day when at some time the dust clouds do not roll over. 'Visibility' approaches zero and every-thing is covered again with a silt-like deposit which may vary in depth from a film to actual ripples on the kitchen floor. I keep oiled cloths on the window sills and between the upper and lower sashes. Some seal the windows with gummed-paper strips used in wrapping parcels, but no method is fully effective . . .

Naturally you will wonder why we stay here where conditions are so disheartening. Why not pick up and leave as so many others have done? Yet I cannot act or think as if the experiences of our 27 years of life had never been. To break all the closely knit ties of our continued and united efforts for the sake of a possibly greater comfort elsewhere seems like defaulting in our task. We may *have* to leave. We can't hold out indefinitely without some income, however small. But if we can keep the taxes paid, we can work and hope for a better day. We long for the garden and little chickens, the trees and birds and wild flowers of the years gone by. Perhaps if we do our part these good things may return some day, for others if not for ourselves.

A great reddish-brown dust cloud is rising now from the southeast, so we must get out and do our night work before it arrives. Our thoughts go with you.

August 11, 1935

We spent the better part of a night during this blistering week trying to save two of the best young cows from the effect of the prussic acid which develops in the stunted sorghum. We thought for a time they would die.

We have had *no* rain for over a month. All hope of an adequate forage crop has now followed into oblivion the earlier hope of wheat and maize production. The cattle stay alive thus far on weeds, but the pastures are destitute of grass. The heat is intense, and the drying winds are practically continuous, with a real 'duster' occurring every few days to keep us humble.

January 28, 1936

Perhaps books on pioneer life with the usual successful outcome have helped to a wrong impression that country people live on game and fish and fruits and in general on the free bounty of heaven. Many people have no idea of the cash expense of operating a farm today. This year we are keeping a separate account of expenses for car, truck and tractor, all of which are old and frequently in need of repair. I fear we shall be discouraged by the close of the year.

March 8, 1936

Nothing that you hear or read will be likely to exaggerate the physical discomfort or material losses due to these storms . . .

I suppose there is something of the gambler in all of us. We instinctively feel that the longer we travel on a straight road, the nearer we must be coming to a turn. People here can't quite believe yet in a hopeless climatic change that would deprive them permanently of the gift of rain.

**Letters from the Dust Bowl**; Caroline A. Henderson; *Reader's Digest*; July, 1936

Now I lay me down to snore,
Tons of dust in every pore.
If another day I do not see,
There'll be no need to bury me.

**The Dust Bowl Song**; Anonymous; 1935

## A MERCILESS SUN AND A SCOURGE OF INSECTS DESTROY CROPS, CATTLE AND MEN—TWO-THIRDS OF THE COUNTRY AFFECTED

Cattle staggered and fell, and did not rise. Toward afternoon the bleating of sheep thinned into silence around empty water holes. In cities men and women stomped along asphalt paving ridged like mud. From rows of shattered grain came the faint munching sound of countless insect jaws. Bells tolled imploringly for prayer.

Withering heat, rushing out of the furnace of the prairie dust bowl, blasted crops, sucked up rivers and lakes, and transformed the nation —from the Rockies to the Atlantic—into a vast simmering cauldron . . .

Of the figurative four horsemen of the plains—heat, drought, hail, and insect pests—two had ridden the prairies this year. Suddenly in Dakota and Montana grasshoppers shadowed the ground as they dropped toward dying fields. When the grain gave out they attacked leafless trees, fence posts, clothing hanging in the backyards. From Nebraska, Gov. Roy Cochran frantically telegraphed for 200 cars of poisoned bran to supplement the 75 cars already received. In Iowa CCC workers mixed poison mash and rushed it off to farms infested with hoppers and chinch bugs. In Arkansas, in Kansas, in Missouri, warfare against the pests went on night and day.

*Newsweek*; July 18, 1936

April 11, 1935

## OKLAHOMA FAMILIES DESERT FARMS

March 23, 1936

## WINDS WHIRL SILT IN WHEAT BELT; MANY ABANDON FARMS

The Dust Bowl is a dying land . . . I have not seen more than two automobiles on the road that parallels the railroad track for a hundred miles or more. I have seen human beings only when passing bleak villages, consisting of a few shacks. Houses empty, yards empty. I have not seen a single child in these ghost-like, pathetic villages. The few people I saw looked like a lost people living in a lost land.

I do not exaggerate when I say that in this country there is now no life for miles upon miles; no human beings, no birds, no animals. Only a dull brown land with cracks showing. Hills furrowed with eroded gullies—you have seen pictures like that in ruins of lost civilizations.

**Unto Dust—**; George Greenfield; *Reader's Digest*; May, 1937

The land just blew away; we had to go somewhere.
Kansas preacher; June, 1936

The cars of the migrant people crawled out of the side roads onto the great cross-country highway, and they took the migrant way to the West. In the daylight they scuttled like bugs to the westward; and as the dark caught them, they clustered like bugs near to a shelter and to water. And because they were lonely and perplexed, because they had all come from places of sadness and worry and defeat, and because they were all going to a new mysterious place, they huddled together; they talked together; they shared their lives, their food, and the things they hoped for in the new country. Thus it might be that one family camped near a spring, and another camped for the spring and for company, and a third because two families had pioneered the place and found it good. And when the sun went down, perhaps twenty families and twenty cars were there.

In the evening a strange thing happened: the twenty families became one family, the children were the children of all. The loss of home became one loss, and the golden time in the West was one dream. And it might be that a sick child threw despair into the hearts of twenty families, of a hundred people; that a birth there in a tent kept a hundred people quiet and awestruck through the night and filled a hundred people with the birth-joy in the morning. A family which the night before had been lost and fearful might search its goods to find a present for the new baby. In the evening, sitting about the fires, the twenty were one . . .

They were not farm men any more, but migrant men. And the thought, the planning, the long staring silence that had gone out to the fields, went now to the roads, to the distance, to the West. That man whose mind had been bound with acres lived with narrow concrete miles. And his thought and his worry were not any more with rainfall, with wind and dust, with the thrust of the crops. Eyes watched tires, ears listened to clattering motors, and minds struggled with oil, with gasoline, with the thinning rubber between air and road. Then a broken gear was a tragedy. Then water in the evening was the yearning, and food over the fire. Then health to go on was the need and strength to go on, and spirit to go on.

**The Grapes of Wrath**; John Steinbeck; 1939

Come live in Southern California for the good of your soul, they used to sing . . . 'Even the tears one sheds in California are tears of gladness.' . . . But now it was different . . . Three or four thousand unbidden guests are arriving monthly fetching with them nothing but the alkali the desert covered them with, the rampageous appetites they couldn't satisfy at home, the remnants of hope that died of the drought and a belief that in California miracles grew.
**California, Here We Come**; Walter Davenport; *Collier's*; August, 1935

'No, we ain't got no money,' Pa said. '—But they's plenty of us to work, an' we're all good men. Get good wages out there an' we'll put 'em together. We'll make out.'
**The Grapes of Wrath**; John Steinbeck

I heard somewheres how California was giving out forty acres and a free house to white Protestants.
Migrant cotton picker; 1935

## OKIES GO HOME: NO RELIEF AVAILABLE IN CALIFORNIA
Billboard on Nevada/California border, 1935

Near Thermal, southeast of Los Angeles, we saw what looked like the advance guard of a Kansas Society picnic—a family of seventeen, thirteen children, parents and grandparents. They had arrived in what might have been a taxicab and a trailer. The trailer, shy two springs and both doors, might, by crowding, have accommodated five smallish persons. The ex-taxicab could have carried four more if they were tough. The family explained that they had taken turns walking. They had been on the road twenty-seven days . . .

They straggled in across the Yuma bridge down in the southeast corner of the state looking much like war-zone refugees. There were a number of disconcerted Californians there, official and otherwise, engaged in the wholly futile business of shooing them off. There was a large, pink, breast-beating lady who, we guessed, was one of those active souls who dedicated their lives to being conspicuously present at all civic betterment demonstrations. She was standing in her motor-car, a handkerchief to her mouth and nose, removing it occasionally to give us the benefit of her mature opinions: 'They probably haven't bathed in weeks. If they persist in coming and are glad to be here why don't they look more cheerful? At least the Japanese are clean . . .'

But far more active at deploring was the young man with the downy, blond mustache. He was dressed in nicely fitting khaki, long trousers, a stiff-brim campaign hat and a Sam Browne. Very erect and primly severe, he addressed the slumped driver of a rolling wreck that screamed from every hinge, bearing and coupling. 'California's relief rolls are overcrowded now. No use to come farther,' he cried.

The half-collapsed driver ignored him—merely turned his head to be sure his numerous family was still with him. They were so tightly wedged in, that escape was impossible. 'There is really nothing for you here,' the neat, trooperish young man went on. 'Nothing, really nothing.'

And the forlorn man on the moaning car looked at him, dull, emotionless, incredibly weary, and said: 'So? Well, you ought to see what they got where I come from.'

Anyway, here they were—at the end of the trail. Yonder swelled the ocean and at their backs the mountains mocked them. The power of illusion that had supported them through dust and flood had spent itself. Now they were ready for a southern California miracle. Here was the land of daily millenniums, the tranquil home of the simple country doctor whose heart bleeds for the old and the weary, the pulpit of Sinclair [Lewis], who still promises to scotch poverty, the Happy Valley of ten thousand patented gospels and incorporated whimwhams designed to warm you with telepathy and fatten you with mumbo-jumbo. And here we saw the straggled thousands waiting in tents and tin-can hovels and even roofless beneath the patient heavens, for the touch of the magic hand.

But up north in Sacramento, angry patriots were urging the adoption of an astonishing law—probably thoroughly unconstitutional —to exclude Americans as well as Japanese from California. Something had to be done, they cried, to stop this invasion of the unemployed of other states . . .

Several of the loudest voices in California . . . were laying the invasion to Red Radicalism and told us chilling stories of how these ragged regiments were being herded into the state on orders from Moscow.

**California, Here We Come**; Walter Davenport; *Collier's*; August 10, 1935

If the Constitution doesn't guarantee citizens the right to breathe the air, walk on the earth, view the sunset, and hunt for a job without a mounted policeman's approval, then we've no Constitution.
*Nevada State Journal*; February 11, 1936

'You'll be campin' by a ditch, you an' fifty other families. An' [a fella] will look in your tent an' see if you got anything lef' to eat. An' if you got nothin', he says, "Wanna job?" An' you'll say, "I sure do, mister. I'll sure thank you for a chance to do some work." An' he'll say, "I can use you." An' you'll say, "When do I start?" An' he'll tell you where to go, an' what time, an' then he'll go on. Maybe he needs two hunderd men, so he talks to five hunderd, an' they tell other folks, an' when you get to the place, they's a thousan' men. This here fella says, "I'm payin' twenty cents an hour." An' maybe half a the men walk off. But they's still five hunderd that's so goddamn hungry they'll work for nothin' but biscuits. Well, this here fella's got a contract to pick them peaches or—chop that cotton. You see now? The more fellas he can get, less he's gonna pay. An' he'll get a fella with kids if he can.'
**The Grapes of Wrath**; John Steinbeck; 1939

The San Joaquin Valley is about 275 miles long and averages some forty miles in width. The big crops are grapes, peaches, apricots, nectarines, and cotton. Probably 90 per cent of the work of harvesting these crops is performed by migratory workers. At least half of these people are former farm owners who, along with their farms, were blown out of the Oklahoma, Arkansas, and Texas dust bowls. They travel in ten-dollar jalopies, carting their women and children along. Because three weeks is a long spell of work to find in one place, they have no homes. Hence they have no votes and are ineligible for relief . . .

Fruit pickers and cotton pickers are paid by quantity. Grapes pay the best. A good grape picker can make $1.25 a day. Earnings in the other crops range from seventy-five cents to a dollar a day. Out of this comes twenty-five cents a day for rent. A 'model cabin' can be erected for $18.75, but practically none exist. The typical migratory

worker's accommodation consists of a tar-paper-shanty with no
plumbing and no floor. He must furnish his own blankets and rustle
his own firewood. At the very large ranches he buys his groceries from
the company store, and the prices are high. Thinning peaches is
another important job, for which top pay on all ranches but one is
$1.25 a day—from which ninety-five cents is subtracted for board.
The children in these wretched families seldom are able to obtain any
schooling, and their mortality rate is appalling . . .

Before someone tries to remark they are lucky to find work in the
San Joaquin and Imperial Valleys to support themselves, let me point
out that without them those lush valleys would soon revert to desert.
Absolutely no other type of labor is available to harvest those
valuable crops. The Mexicans and Filipinos fled from the San Joaquin
Valley three years ago: couldn't endure the low standard of living.
Only 100 per cent American can stand the gaff there.

**California's Blackshirts**; Paul Y. Anderson; *Nation*; August 6, 1938

That old dust storm killed my baby,
Can't kill me, Lord, can't kill me.
That old dust storm got my family,
Can't get me, Lord, can't get me.

That old landlord took my homestead,
Can't get me, Lord, can't get me.
That old dry spell killed my crops, boys,
Can't kill me, no, can't kill me.

That old pawnshop got my furniture,
Can't get me, Lord, can't get me.
That old dust storm would of blown my farm down,
Can't get me, Lord, can't get me.

That old dust storm might kill my wheat, boys,
Can't kill me, no, can't kill me.
That old wind might blow this world down,
But it can't blow me down, Lord, can't kill me.
**Dust Can't Kill Me**; song; Woody Guthrie

Federal Resettlement Administration office

YEARS OF DUST

RESETTLEMENT ADMINISTRATION
Rescues Victims
Restores Land to Proper Use

January 23, 1937

## 150,000 HOMELESS IN FLOOD; 22 DIE AS WATERS RISE IN 12 STATES

Practically all schools in the state of Kentucky were closed as highways became impassable. Coal mines were abandoned as flood waters poured into their shafts. All public utilities in Louisville were threatened.

National Guardsmen were mobilized to police the city after police and firemen had been sent into the flood areas to aid rescue and relief workers. Militiamen were also called out in Ohio, Indiana and Tennessee.

Failure of water-logged equipment in utility plants plunged more than a score of communities into darkness. Snow, sleet, and freezing weather added to the distress of many refugees sheltered in box cars, public buildings, churches and tents.

*New York Times*

January 26, 1937

## 104 DIE IN FLOOD; CITIES IN CHAOS; 600,000 FLEE

As the water rose in the Frankfort [Kentucky] Reformatory, 2,900 panic-stricken prisoners began fighting. First everybody fought the guards, 25 swimming out into the river and 24 swimming back when shots were fired over their heads. Then the Negroes fought the whites. National Guardsmen withdrew outside the prison walls, announcing that twelve prisoners were dead and that all had 'absolutely gone mad.'

*Time*; February 1, 1937

February 3, 1937

## WON'T FLEE UNTIL TOLD WHAT EVACUATE MEANS

When it's lightning my mind gets frightened,
My nerves begin weakening down,
My nerves begin weakening down.
And the shack where we was living begin moving 'round.

Women and children was screaming, saying,
'Lord where must we go?
'Lord where must we go?
'The flood water has broke the levees and we ain't safe here no more.'

When it begins, clouds dark as midnight,
Keep raining all the time,
Keep raining all the time.
I say, 'Oh; I wonder why the sun don't ever shine.'
And the way it keeps raining, it's driving me out of my mind.

**Flood Water**; song; Lonnie Johnson; 1937

January 30, 1937

## DISASTER ENGULFS OHIO VALLEY AND SWEEPS SOUTHWARD; PRESIDENT MOBILIZES MILITARY AND CIVIL FORCES FOR RELIEF

It was like an orange going down an ostrich's neck. Fortnight ago it was up at Wheeling, Portsmouth, Cincinnati. Last week it moved slowly down through Louisville and Evansville to Cairo. But the Ohio River, unlike an ostrich's neck, remained swollen after the orange passed, for floods recede slowly.

**Ohio River flood scenes, 1937**

On the national map it was only a little puddle, but to Army planes flying succor, it looked like a shoreless yellow sea studded here and there with tree tops and half submerged buildings. To people crouching on house roofs, it was an immeasurable amount of ugly yellow water surging higher and higher hours without end . . .

Saddest of all was Louisville, Ky. which has virtually no hills. Three-fourths of the city, at flood crest, were inundated. Its business and residential districts alike were in water, its Negro shanties and mansions of the rich. Its electricity was off, its power-station partly submerged in the yellow flood. Over 230,000 Louisville people were homeless, at least 200 dead (no official figures), few of them by drowning, most from exposure. Property loss was estimated at $100,000,000 . . .

At week's end the Red Cross announced that it was already caring for 676,176 homeless people, was operating 360 concentration camps, 108 field hospitals, had 380 trained disaster relief workers and 1,215 nurses in the field. But such figures became obsolete almost as soon as issued. The Coast Guard established headquarters at Evansville, Ind., brought 225 of its boats on the scene for rescue work, sent for nearly 200 more from points as far distant as Boston. It had 15 airplanes in action. The U.S. Public Health Service was busy shipping anti-typhoid and smallpox vaccine, diphtheria antitoxin, influenza and pneumonia serum; was mobilizing a corps of sanitary engineers to face new problems as the flood recedes.

*Time*; February 8, 1937

February 2, 1937
## FLOOD BABY NAMED NOAH BECAUSE OF HIS SURVIVAL

The recent flood took Finley Johnson's piano away, but it brought back another just as good.

Finley's home is in the Birds Point-New Madrid floodway. When the basin was inundated last month his piano started floating around, banging out windows and spreading general havoc, so 'I opened the doors, shoved the piano out, and saw it float away,' he said today.

'Imagine my surprise when I returned to my home and found another piano had floated in through the open doors during the flood.'
*New York Times*; February 23, 1937

Pop, I've found our house. It's three miles down the river, against some trees, and upside down. Everything's in it, but what a mess!
Paducah, Kentucky boy; February, 1937

The flood is over. Now the anxious townspeople can leave their temporary roosts atop the hills on the city's rim. They struggle back to their homes—and to chaos.

The town is soaking under a layer of oozing mud and dripping rubbish. Here beside a grimy piano with swollen, rigid keys lies the carcass of a horse. There stands a splintered telephone pole enmeshed in chicken wires, leaves and straw. Everywhere there is shattered glass, for thousands of windows in town have been crushed by the water's force.

The marching waters have stripped the bridge of its tar-block pavement, leaving a naked super-structure. They have jerked huge slabs of concrete off the highway. They have undermined the side-walks, either shattering the heavy flagstones or tossing them out of position . . .

Down the street is the Griffin house—once white, but now, from the ground to the second floor, a muddy brown. Half of the fence around the yard is rusted and distorted; the other half washed away. In front of the house is a pile of tangled wood, a wicker chair, a sofa matted with talc-fine silt, a table, a battered shed. None of the articles belong to the Griffins. Neighbors will drop by soon to claim them.

In the parlor, one of the Griffin boys is playing the hose on the walls and ceiling. The jet of water dissolves a two-inch layer of mud; and a silt-laden stream flows along the ridges of the buckled hardwood floor and out into the hall. Hosing is the only way of throwing off the flood's residue . . .

A neighbor calls to announce that he found the Griffin back steps down the street and tagged them. Another gossips about the troubles of the Red Cross. Among the unidentified bodies that have been recovered are a dozen dressed in more formal clothes than those worn by most of the victims. A graveyard has been washed out.

Outside the town, of course, the waters have carried off not only homes and livestock, but acres of rich, planted farmland as well. Some of this latter has been deposited where the Griffin lawn used to be. There will be no lawn next June: instead will sprout a botanical potpourri of hollyhocks, corn, cabbages.

When the rampant waters of the Ohio or the Mississippi or the Cumberland or the Little Miami fall back below their levees, Mrs. Griffin and her neighbors invariably return to what was once home—though they know that in coming years they will again hear the dreaded cry, 'To the hills!'
**After the Deluge**; Thomas Kramer; *Reader's Digest*; March, 1937

**Flood aftermath and relief operations**

When all the world is a hopeless jumble,
And the rain drops tumble all around,
Heaven opens up a magic lane.
When all the clouds darken up the skyway,
There's a rainbow to be found
Leading from your windowpane.
To a place behind the sun,
Just a step beyond the rain.

Somewhere over the rainbow way up high,
There's a land that I dreamed of, once in a lullaby;
Somewhere over the rainbow, skies are blue,
And the dreams that you dare to dream really do come true.

Someday I'll wish upon a star
And wake up where the clouds are far behind me.
Where troubles melt like lemon drops, away,
Above the chimney-tops, that's where you'll find me.

Somewhere over the rainbow bluebirds fly,
Birds fly over the rainbow, why then,
Oh why can't I?
**Over the Rainbow**; song; Harburg & Arlen; 1939

Do not look at the Negro.

His earthly problems are ended.

Instead, look at the seven WHITE children who gaze at this gruesome spectacle.

Is it horror or gloating on the face of the neatly dressed seven-year-old girl on the right?

Is the tiny four-year-old on the left old enough, one wonders, to comprehend the barbarism her elders have perpetrated?

Rubin Stacy, the Negro, who was lynched at Fort Lauderdale, Florida, on July 19, 1935, for "threatening and frightening a white woman," suffered PHYSICAL torture for a few short hours. But what psychological havoc is being wrought in the minds of the white children? Into what kinds of citizens

# WORLDS IN COLLISION

will they grow up? What kind of America will they help to make after being familiarized with such an inhuman, law-destroying practice as lynching?

The manacles, too, tell their own story. The Negro was powerless in the hands of the law, but the law was just as powerless to protect him from being lynched. Since 1922 over one-half the lynched victims have been taken from legal custody. Less than one percent of the lynchers have been punished, and they very lightly. More than 5,000 such instances of lynching have occurred without any punishment whatever, establishing beyond doubt that federal legislation is necessary, as in the case of kidnapping, to supplement state action.

What, you may ask, can YOU do?

In May, 1935, a filibuster in the United States Senate, led by a small group of senators, most of them from the states with the worst lynching record, succeeded in side-tracking the Costigan-Wagner Anti-Lynching Bill. This bill will be brought up again in the 1936 session of Congress.

1. Write to your Congressmen and to the two United States Senators from your state urging them to work assiduously and vote for passage of the bill.

2. Get the church, lodge or other fraternal organization, social club, and whatever other groups you belong to to pass resolutions urging Congressmen and Senators from your state to vote for the bill.

3. Write letters to your newspapers and magazines urging their help.

4. Make as generous a contribution as you can to the organization which for twenty-five years has fought this evil and which is acting as a coordinating agent of church, labor, fraternal and other groups, with a total membership of 42,000,000, which are working for passage of the Costigan-Wagner Bill.

THE NATIONAL ASSOCIATION FOR THE
ADVANCEMENT OF COLORED PEOPLE
69 Fifth Avenue, New York

- - - - - - - - - - - - - - - - - - - - - - - - - - - - - - - - - - - - - - - - - - - - - -

N.A.A.C.P.
69 Fifth Avenue, New York

Here is my contribution of $........... for the fight against lynching.

Name_____

Address_____

City_____

State_____

Will Walker was shot to death a month ago on the streets of Bartow, Georgia; Ernest Bell was beaten to death with an iron pipe and his body thrown into a well near Bartow; and an unidentified man about thirty-five years of age was shot in the head and breast six times and, apparently because he did not die quickly enough, his head was almost severed from his body with a knife. The body was found in a a field near Bartow.

Sam Outler would be dead now, too, if Sheriff Jim Smith had not put him in the Jefferson county jail for protection against the gang of white men who killed the three others. Sam sits in his cell, his head swollen and sore from the beating he received the night his friend Ernest Bell was lynched.

You can climb the cell block stairs and find Sam Outler sitting on his iron bunk waiting—he does not know what he's waiting for, and after you have talked to him a while, you yourself begin to wonder what there is for him to wait for. If Sam goes back to Bartow, he will be killed. If he leaves the state, his family will never see him again. And so, while you sit there looking at Sam and listening to him, you cannot help feeling uncomfortable; because your skin is white, and Sam Outler is an accusing finger pointing at the white men of your country who butcher hogs with more humaneness than they kill Negroes.

Last night I revisited Bartow, Georgia. It was not quite midnight when I got there. The town appeared to be as peaceful as the starry sky overhead. There were lights in some of the big white houses on the hill above the stores and railway station. Two or three men were hurrying along the streets. A night watchman sat on the steps of a ginnery. Behind the town the South Branch of the Ogeechee River flowed as smoothly and as silently as a stream of crude oil. Hoar frost was forming on the roofs of buildings bordering the lowlands of the river.

Walking up the unpaved main street that had dried out after a week of rain, you cannot help stopping in front of the drug store and looking at the window display. Costly cosmetics and cheap ones are piled side by side, and behind them all is a seven-color cardboard poster displaying three naked girls and the name of a perfume manufacturer. All around you are signs repeating the magic phrase: 'Drink Coca-Cola.' You move on before the aromatic drug store smell gains possession of your senses . . .

I stood on the road, listening to sounds in the Ogeechee swamps to the right and left and in the rear, and watching the lights of the town spread over the hillside, and I could not forget what Sam Outler had said. He was speaking of the night he was beaten with the pipe and Ernest Bell was thrown into the well.

'The white men came up to where we was and said Ernest was a son-of-a-bitch. Ernest told them, "White-folks, I ain't no son-of-a-bitch, and I don't want to be called one." Then this young Bradley boy steps out and hits Ernest with something he had in his hand, and Ernest told him not to do that no more.

'Then I said, "Look here, white-folks, me and Ernest don't want to make trouble." Some of the white men went to a automobile and took some short pieces of iron pipes out and came back where we was. I heard Ernest saying to them, "I don't mind being called any other name you can think of, but don't call me a son-of-a-bitch." Just then I saw them coming at us, and the next thing I knew was the next day. I reckon the only reason why they didn't shoot me and throw me in the well with Ernest was because I didn't do much talking like Ernest did. I saw that Bradley boy run up and hit Ernest on the head with the pipe, and that's the last I remember, because somebody started beating me on the head with the other pipes about the same time.' . . .

The Negro whose mutilated body was found in a field near Bartow today lies buried in an unmarked grave in an abandoned field. Nobody knows his name; nobody cares. But the men who killed him, like those who killed Ernest Bell and Will Walker, walk the streets in heroic strides. Their names are known; they will even boast of their crimes. But the coroner's jury washed its hands of the deeds when it returned the verdict: 'Death at the hands of parties unknown.' . . .

Two weeks ago Will Jordan was killed by two white men who went to his house after midnight and shot him while he was asleep in bed with his wife. His six children were in the room with him. The next day the two men admitted that they had killed the wrong Negro— they were after someone else and had gone into the Jordan house by mistake. The killers were acquitted. They promised they would kill the 'right' Negro the next time they went out shooting.

But this killing took place in another section of Jefferson County. I was standing in the main street of Bartow trying to wonder what I was doing there. I was trying to reason why three Negroes could be put to death in such a quiet, peaceful town by white men who were at that moment in their homes asleep. Nobody was disturbed. Nobody was walking around in the dark with a flashlight trying to find evidence to convict the killers. Nobody was abroad offering protection to Negroes who wished to come out of their cabins. Bartow was as calm as any Georgia town at midnight. Georgia was as peaceful as any other Southern state in January . . . I walked once more up the street and looked at the display of perfumes, soaps, and powders in the drug store window. The drug store odor again filtered through my senses . . .

Half a mile from the main street, on the Augusta highway, I stopped and looked for a while at the swollen and bloated carcass of a mule that had been killed by an automobile or truck. The mule was lying on the shoulder of the highway, and it appeared to have been dead a week or ten days. It will probably remain there until the swamp rats and buzzards finish removing it bite by bite . . .

Back in Augusta in the early hours of the morning, I stop and enter a drug store for a pack of cigarettes, and the startling odor of perfumes and cosmetics does something to me. The clerk thinks I am drunk; I am unable to ask for what I wish, and I have to cling to the tobacco counter for support. He takes me by the arm and leads me to the sidewalk, and with a gentle shove, starts me on my way. Partly revived by the night air, I realize that, after a night spent in the Ogeechee swamps, perfumery and brutality will ever plague me.
**Parties Unknown in Georgia**; Erskine Caldwell; *New Masses*; January 23, 1934

## SOUTHERN SENATORS FILIBUSTER
Last week Senator Ellison D. Smith of South Carolina and a handful of Southern colleagues concocted a full-fledged filibuster against the Wagner-Costigan Anti-Lynching Bill which would penalize sheriffs who fail to protect their prisoners from mobs. The bill would also allow families of lynch victims to recover $2,000 to $10,000 from county governments. Eight aroused, eloquent Senators vowed 'it shall not pass' . . . They promised to filibuster till the cows come home, rather than allow the Senate to debate the Anti-Lynching Bill.
*Newsweek*; March 4, 1935

May 2, 1935

## LYNCHING BILL IS DROPPED; SIX-DAY FILIBUSTER ENDS

I did not choose the tools with which I must work. But I've got to get legislation passed by Congress to save America. The Southerners by reason of the seniority rule in Congress are chairmen or occupy strategic places on most of the Senate and House committees. If I come out for the Anti-Lynching Bill now, they will block every bill I ask Congress to pass to keep America from collapsing. I just can't take that risk.
FDR to Walter White of NAACP; 1935

November 16, 1937

## NEW LYNCHING BILL IS MET BY THREAT OF FILIBUSTER

November 20, 1937

## SENATORS CONTINUE ANTI-LYNCH FILIBUSTER AMID ANGRY CLASHES

Harlem is from 55 to 60 percent unemployed. Many of its inhabitants, before the depression, were employed as house servants or as attendants in hotels. Others worked in the building trades, as elevator men, as waiters and dishwashers in restaurants. Not all Harlem Negroes, contrary to the impression to be gained from a number of novels, are orchestra leaders and night-club entertainers. They have been hit perhaps harder than any other group in New York. Many of them have not had work in four years.

Relief has been inadequate. Charges have been made that it is one-third lower in Harlem than elsewhere. Some unemployed Negroes say they have to wait days, and some say weeks, before getting assistance. Relief administration has been entirely in the hands of white persons whose knowledge and understanding of the Negro is limited. White investigators have caused much antagonism and bad feeling. There have been quarrels and recriminations and, in some instances, fist-fights and brawls.

**The Riot in Harlem**; Hamilton Basso; *New Republic*; April 3, 1935

March 20, 1935

## POLICE SHOOT INTO RIOTERS; KILL NEGRO IN HARLEM MOB

In midafternoon, Lino Rivera, a 16-year-old Puerto Rican, strolled through a Harlem 5-and-10-cent store: 'I saw a knife that attracted me and I walked up and took it.' A sharp-eyed floor-walker nabbed him. The youth struggled. Another storeman walked up and snarled: 'Let's take him downstairs and beat the hell out of him.'

Without hurting him, the store officials let the boy out a basement door. But a young Negress, overhearing the threats, screamed: 'They're beating that boy! They're killing him!'

A crowd milled sullenly outside the store. Then a hearse appeared. No one in the street knew definitely why it parked at the rear entrance of the 5-and-10-cent store. But the mob jumped to conclusions. The boy had been killed.

Within an hour, members of the Young Liberators, a radical youths' organization, began haranguing crowds from soap-boxes. The mob took up the chant: 'White men killed a colored boy!' Communist sympathizers passed out inflammatory handbills, the spark that fired the tinder.

The cauldron boiled over. Marauding bands of Negroes roamed the country's largest Negro settlement. White folk scurried for cover. Those found on the streets got pummeled.

The Negro weapons consisted of kitchen knives, bricks, paving blocks, razors and old pistols.

Lewis J. Valentine, New York's stern Police Commissioner, centered 500 uniformed police, 200 plain-clothes men, and 50 radio cars in the colored colony. Berserk Negroes smashed windows of 200 stores and walked off with stolen goods. Dealers estimated the loss at $300,000.

When the officers tried to stop the wholesale looting, the attack turned on them. Detectives with gashed heads staggered into ambulances. Blacks, crouching behind roof parapets, sniped at patrolmen.

Casualties: two dead; scores carted to hospitals with serious injuries.

*Newsweek*; March 30, 1935

One Negro, in discussing the affair, said he was surprised that trouble had not broken out before this. It had been brewing for a long time. The chance apprehension of a boy, the spread of a rumor that seemed to have a basis in fact, was the only accident that set off the anger of a section of society that has suffered through five years of depression.

**The Riot in Harlem**; Hamilton Basso; *New Republic*; April 3, 1935

**Huey Long**

I'm a small fish here in Washington. But I'm the Kingfish to the folks down in Louisiana.
Huey Long; 1932

Huey has been accused of practically all the crimes in the category, but he has managed to lick his enemies at every turn. He became not only Governor, but also Senator, and the undisputed boss of Louisiana. Today he is really a one-man machine. His red hair always seems to get redder as he works himself up to fighting speed, and his five feet ten inches bristle with limitless energy. He is a smart politician for all his eccentricities. He brooks no interference and takes no advice. Nor is there any detail too small or unimportant for him to give it his personal attention. He is, in brief, the State of Louisiana.
**The Louisiana Kingfish**; L. Cochran; *American Mercury*; July, 1932

I was elected railroad commissioner in Louisiana in nineteen hundred and eighteen, and they tried to impeach me in nineteen hundred and twenty. But they failed to impeach me in nineteen hundred and twenty so they indicted me in nineteen hundred and twenty-one. And then when I wiggled through that I managed to become Governor in nineteen hundred and twenty-eight . . . and they impeached me in nineteen hundred and twenty-nine.
Huey Long to Senate; 1935

In a radio address tonight Senator Long declared that there was no further hope from the Roosevelt policies, and urged the American people to join in the Long 'Share Our Wealth' and 'Every Man a King' programs.

His predictions as to economic conditions in 1933 and 1934 had all come true, the Senator declared, justifying his saying, 'I told you so.' . . .

Senator Long said he 'begged and pleaded and did everything else under the sun' to 'try to get Mr. Roosevelt to keep his word that he gave us.' He asserted that he had 'warned the President' what would happen if the 'promises' were not kept.

'Hope for more through Roosevelt? He has promised and promised, smiled and bowed; he has read fine speeches and told anyone in need to get in touch with him. What has it meant? . . .

'When I saw him spending all his time of ease and recreation with the business partners of Mr. John D. Rockefeller, Jr., with such men as the Astors, etc., maybe I ought to have had better sense than to have believed he would ever break down their big fortunes to give enough to the masses to end poverty.

'Maybe some will think me weak for ever believing it at all, but millions of other people were fooled the same as myself.

'All the people of America have been invited to a barbecue. God invited us all to come and eat and drink all we wanted. He smiled on our land and we grew crops of plenty to eat and wear.

'He showed us the earth, the iron and other things to make anything we wanted. He unfolded to us the secrets of science so that our work might be easy. God called: "Come to my feast."

'Then what happened? Rockefeller, Morgan and their crowd stepped up and took enough for 120,000,000 people and left only enough for 5,000,000, for all the 125,000,000 to eat. And so many millions must go hungry and without these good things God gave us unless we call on them to put some of it back.

'I call on you to organize Share Out Wealth societies.'
*New York Times*; January 10, 1935

Although the Share Our Wealth program is excessively simple, its simplicity does not imply clarity. There are two focal objectives. One is to 'give every man, woman and child in the United States five thousand dollars,' with a home, a job, a radio and an automobile to boot for every family. The other is to prohibit great fortunes by restricting the amount of money any man may have or bequeath. The manner in which the second objective can be attained is obvious. Huey has never been averse to excessive taxation so long as the tax is not placed directly upon the rural and small-town voter.
*New Republic*; February 13, 1935

**Every Man a King**
Why weep or slumber, America, Land of brave and true?
With castles, clothing, and food for all, All belongs to you.
Every man a king, every man a king.
For you can be a millionaire.
But there's something belongs to others,
There's enough for all people to share.
When it's sunny June and December too,
Or in the wintertime or spring.
There'll be peace without end
Every neighbor a friend
With every man a king.
Huey Long; song; 1935

May 28, 1935
**SUPREME COURT UNANIMOUSLY RULES NRA AND CODES VOID; ENTIRE CODE STRUCTURE OF NRA INVALIDATED; ROOSEVELT'S POWERS CURBED**

I raise my hand in reverence to the Supreme Court that saved this nation from fascism . . . I thank God that the Supreme Court of the United States does not forget that there is a constitution written in times of stress, under the benignity of Heaven to save the institutions of America from the raids of the Huns and the expedients of the mongrels.
Huey Long; June 2, 1935

## NRA FILIBUSTER BY LONG RUNS THROUGH THE NIGHT; IN 15th HOUR AT 4 A.M.

The full force of the Roosevelt administration was pitted against the lung power of Senator Long of Louisiana in the early hours this morning in a final showdown in the Senate . . .

Administration efforts to save at least the outline of the NRA were suffering an ignominious setback as the result of a filibuster instituted by Mr. Long at 12:15 PM yesterday and which at 3 o'clock this morning was still going strong under the propulsion of the apparently inexhaustible speaking powers of the man from the Louisiana cane-breaks . . .

Hoarse of voice, and forced to jump up and down in setting up exercises to keep his tired limbs awake, the Louisianan was still able to outshout the heckling of the administration Senators and a new coalition among the Senate 'freshmen,' led by Senator Schwellenbach, the arch liberal from Washington.

He was still able to carry on what he termed 'the last stand for the Lord and the Constitution.' He had sipped one glass of milk after another, eaten candy, and nibbled at a sandwich, having been unable to eat either luncheon or dinner . . .

Senator Schwellenbach, spokesman for the 'freshman' group, served open notice on Senator Long that they had been solidified in a movement to see that the 'circus' should not be repeated.

Administration forces proposed to sit out the filibuster if it took until Sunday night, June 16, expiration date of the National Recovery Act.

They felt that this was the only way to deal with Mr. Long, and their precedent for this belief was the fact that 3 weeks ago they let him talk until he almost dropped in his place, and he was not heard from again until yesterday . . .

Senator Long sent out for some chocolate caramels shortly before midnight, and proceeded with speaking and eating at the same time. He washed down the caramels with milk, then paused for a moment to pitch a few of his candies to Senators sitting about him, particularly those who had voted with him earlier in the day.

A few minutes later a faithful secretary slipped a sandwich onto his desk. The Senator would walk over to the plate, break off a small piece of the sandwich, roll it into a small ball and put it into his mouth without missing a word.

As the Senator finished his 11th hour of filibustering he had just completed a 30 minute description of how to make Roquefort cheese salad dressing.

He spent most of the time telling how to stir it. He was admonishing the Senate never to eat it on anything but lettuce, and head lettuce at that, when a question from a Senator started him on another personal attack against President Roosevelt.

*New York Times*; June 13, 1935

We are not going to let Huey Long continue to use the Senate as a medium for making himself the Fascist dictator of America . . . There will be no compromise.

Senator Schwellenbach; June 13, 1935

June 15, 1935

## SKELETON NRA IS EXTENDED

I don't know when they're going to hold the Democratic convention. Why don't they hold the Democratic convention and the Communist convention together and save money . . . Under Roosevelt there is no more any Democratic party—there is a New Deal party, a combination of the Stalin and Hitler systems, with a dash of Italian Fascism.
Huey Long; July 26; 1935

August 14, 1935
## HUEY LONG TO SEEK PRESIDENCY IN 1936; WITH HIS MAIN GOAL TO 'BEAT ROOSEVELT'

As God is my judge, the only way they will keep your friend Huey Long from the White House is to kill him.
Rev. Gerald L. K. Smith; 1935

September 9, 1935
## DOCTOR SHOOTS HUEY LONG IN LOUISIANA STATE CAPITOL
Twenty years of newspaper experience failed to prepare me for the tragedy I witnessed Sunday night.

I was coming out of Governor Allen's office when I heard a shot. Outside in the hall I noticed Senator Long staggering away, clasping his side with his right hand. Half a dozen other members of the Senator's guard joined in the shooting and the man who shot Senator Long pitched forward, dead from thirty or forty bullets.

Senator Long, meanwhile, walked down the hall, descended the stairs, was aided to an automobile and taken to the nearby Ladyville Sanitorium.
Charles Frampton, eyewitness; September, 1935

September 10, 1935
## SENATOR HUEY LONG DIES OF WOUNDS AFTER THIRTY-HOUR FUTILE FIGHT FOR LIFE

**To All Hearst Editors and Universal Service Bureaus:**
The Chief instructs that the phrase 'Soak the Successful' be used in all references to the administration's tax program instead of the phrase 'Soak the Thrifty' hitherto used, also he wants the words 'Raw Deal' used instead of 'New Deal.'
E. D. Coblentz, Hearst Newspaper Syndicate; 1935

June 19, 1936
## ROOSEVELT NOMINATED BY DEMOCRATS FOR SECOND TERM

In the summer of 1933, a nice old gentleman wearing a silk hat fell off the end of the pier. He was unable to swim. A friend ran down the pier, dived overboard, and pulled him out; but the silk hat floated off with the tide. After the old gentleman had been revived, he was effusive in his thanks. He praised his friend for saving his life. Today, three years later, the old gentleman is berating his friend because the silk hat was lost.
Franklin D. Roosevelt; campaign speech; 1936

June 12, 1936
## REPUBLICAN CHOICE FOR PRESIDENT IS ALF LANDON OF KANSAS

I accept the nomination of the Republican Party for the Presidency of the United States . . .

The present administration asked for, and received, extraordinary powers upon the assurance that these were to be temporary . . .

Now it becomes our duty to examine the record as it stands. The record shows that the [Roosevelt] measures did not fit together in any definite program of recovery. Many of them worked at cross-purposes and defeated themselves . . . As a result recovery has been set back again and again. Judged by the things that make us a nation of happy families, the New Deal has fallen far short of success . . .

The time has come to stop fumbling with recovery. American initiative is not a commodity to be delivered in pound packages through a governmental bureau. It is a vital force in the life of our nation and it must be freed! . . .

This then is the most important question before us: Shall we continue to delegate more and more power to the Chief Executive or do we desire to preserve the American form of government? . . .

The Republican Party proposes to maintain a free competitive system—a system under which, and only under which, can there be independence, equality and opportunity, and work for all.

Kansas Governor Alf Landon; July 23, 1936

Let me warn you and warn the nation against the smooth evasion which says, 'Of course we believe all these things; we believe in social security; we believe in work for the unemployed; we believe in saving homes. Cross our hearts and hope to die, we believe in all these things; but we do not like the way the present administration is doing them. Just turn them over to us. We will do all of them—we will do more of them—we will do them better; and, most important of all, the doing of them will not cost anybody anything.'

Franklin D. Roosevelt; campaign speech; 1936

The great betrayer and liar, Franklin D. Roosevelt, who promised to drive the money changers from the temple, has succeeded [only] in driving the farmers from their homesteads and the citizens from their homes in the cities . . .

It is most significant, my friends, that the hand of Moscow backs the Communist leaders in America, and aims to pledge their support for Franklin Delano Roosevelt where Communism stands.

Does Democracy mean that we shall fail?

Is it Democracy for the President of this nation to assume power over Congress and to insist that his 'must' legislation be passed? Is that Democracy?

Or is it Democracy for the President of the United States to say: 'Pass this legislation whether it is constitutional or not.' Is that Democracy? . . .

I ask you to purge the man who claims to be a Democrat, from the Democratic Party, and I mean Franklin Double-Crossing Roosevelt.
Father Charles Coughlin; July, 1936

For twelve years this nation was afflicted with hear-nothing, see-nothing, do-nothing government. The nation looked to the government but the government looked away. Nine mocking years with the golden calf and three long years of the scourge! Nine crazy years at the ticker and three long years in the breadlines! Nine mad years of mirage and three long years of despair! Powerful influences strive today to restore that kind of government, with its doctrine that that government is best which is most indifferent . . .

Never before in our history have these forces been so united against one candidate as they stand today. They are unanimous in their hatred for me—and I welcome their hatred.
Franklin D. Roosevelt; final campaign speech, 1936

November 4, 1936
**ROOSEVELT SWEEPS NATION IN RECORD LANDSLIDE VICTORY**

My voice tonight will be the voice of millions of men and women employed in America's industries; heretofore unorganized, economically exploited and inarticulate. I speak for the Committee for Industrial Organization, which has honored me with its chairmanship and with which are associated twelve great National and International Unions. These unions have a membership in excess of one million persons, who to a greater or lesser degree enjoy the privileges of self-organization and collective bargaining. They reflect adequately the sentiment, hopes and aspirations of those thirty million additional Americans employed in the complex processes of our domestic economy who heretofore have been denied by industry and finance the privilege of collective organization and collective participation in the arbitrary fixation of their economic status. Let him doubt who will that tonight I portray the ceaseless yearning of their hearts and the ambitions of their minds. Let him who will, be he economic tyrant or sordid mercenary, pit his strength against this mighty upsurge of human sentiment now being crystallized in the hearts of thirty millions of workers who clamor for the establishment of industrial democracy and for participation in its tangible fruits.
John L. Lewis radio speech; July 6, 1936

John L. Lewis

I am a union woman
Just as brave as I can be;
I do not like the bosses
And the bosses don't like me.

Join the CIO
Come join the CIO.

I was raised in old Kentucky,
In Kentucky borned and bred;
And when I joined the union,
They called me a Rooshian Red.

If you want to get your freedom,
Also your liberty,
Join the dear old CIO,
Also the ILD.

The bosses ride big fine horses,
While we walk in the mud,
Their banner is the dollar sign,
And ours is striped in blood.

Join the CIO
Come join the CIO.

**I Am a Union Woman**; song; Aunt Molly Jackson

**Flint Auto Workers' strike, 1937**

January 4, 1937

## AUTO UNION VOTES A GENERAL STRIKE IN 69 GENERAL MOTORS COMPANY PLANTS; CIO PLEDGES ITS SUPPORT

The one issue that has prevented a conference between the heads of the General Motors Corporation and the leaders of the United Automobile Workers is the 'sit-down,' or the presence of strikers in the plants . . .

The advantages of the sit-down to the union are sufficiently obvious to anyone familiar with strike tactics. In order to operate the machinery with strikebreakers it is necessary for the employer to get the strikers out of the building. What may under certain circumstances be even more important in terms of morale, it is necessary to get them out even to create the impression that the machinery is being operated, or not improperly operated. In an ordinary strike the first necessity is merely to convoy strikebreakers in sufficient numbers past the plant gates. But it is more difficult to get unwilling men out of a building than it is to disperse pickets from a certain area in the street. The violence involved, even if the operation should be successful, would be more likely to endanger the company's property. Moreover, it is not easy in such a case to maintain that the strikers are the aggressors, so far as the use of violence is concerned. The ordinary technique of the strikebreaking agency, which involves the use of gangsters, machine guns and tear gas, is not adequate to the new situation. In addition, the solidarity of the strikers is more easily maintained while they are continually together than if they were scattered except for periodic meetings or strike duty.

**The Sit Down**; *New Republic*; January 20, 1937

When they tie the can
To a union man,
Sit down, Sit down!
When they give him the sack,
They'll take him back.
Sit down, Sit down!

Sit down, just take a seat,
Sit down, and rest your feet,
Sit down, you've got 'em beat.
Sit down, Sit down!
**Sit Down**; song; Maurice Sugar

January 12, 1937

## 24 HURT IN FLINT STRIKE RIOT; POLICE BATTLE STREET MOBS: TROOPS READY AS AUTO STRIKERS IN PLANT REPEL GAS ATTACK

A hundred of us started walking through the plant calling a sit-down. The company police and thugs sprung up from nowhere. They kept them shut up in the employment office and sprung them loose on us. In a moment there was fighting everywhere. Fighters were rolling on the floor. They had clubs and we were unarmed. They started shooting off tear gas. I saw one fellow hit on the head and when he swung backwards he cut his head on the machinery. He started to stagger out. Two of the thugs knocked him down again. I let go on a couple of thugs. You kind of go crazy when you see thugs beating up men you know.
Striker in Flint plant, 1937

We had to break windows, I tell you, to get air to the boys who were being gassed inside. We don't want violence. We just want to protect our husbands and we are going to.
Wife of striker at Flint, 1937

March 14, 1937

## CHRYSLER STRIKE LARGEST SIT-DOWN

April 23, 1937

## BUICK PLANT WORKERS SIT-DOWN

May 27, 1937

## FORD MEN BEAT AND ROUT LEWIS UNION ORGANIZERS; 16 HURT IN BATTLE; FORD PROPERTY CLEARED

The affair was deliberately provoked by union officials . . . They simply wanted to trump up a charge of Ford brutality that they could take down to Washington and flaunt before the Senatorial [Civil Liberties] Committee . . .

  I would be glad to testify before an official investigating committee and I would have no trouble convincing them that the union cold-bloodedly framed and planned today's disturbance.
Harry H. Bennett; Ford personnel dept.; May 26, 1937

It was the worst licking I've ever taken. They bounced us down the concrete steps of an overpass we had climbed. Then they would knock us down, stand us up, and knock us down again . . . If Mr. Ford thinks this will stop us, he's got another think coming. We'll go back there with enough men to lick him at his own game.
Richard Frankensteen; United Auto Workers; May 26, 1937

Collective bargaining in our shops,
C-I-C-I-O
And in our shops it makes us strong,
C-I-C-I-O.

When the strike is done and we have won,
C-I-C-I-O
We'll hang the scabs all one by one,
C-I-C-I-O.

Our boys are sitting in the shops,
C-I-C-I-O
And they won't come out 'til the speed-up stops,
C-I-C-I-O.

As the years go drifting by
C-I-C-I-O
The auto union will not die
C-I-C-I-O.

With a union here and a union there;
With a scab, scab here and a scab, scab there;
With a sit-down here and a sit-down there;
With a union here and a union there:
Collective bargaining in our shops,
C-I-C-I-O.

**Collective Bargaining in our Shops**; song; Vic Bush

May 26, 1937
## STRIKE AT 5 MILLS OF REPUBLIC STEEL

May 27, 1937
## WALKOUT STARTS PEACEFULLY—COMPANIES REFUSE TO SIGN CONTRACTS WITH CIO

May 31, 1937
## 4 KILLED, 83 HURT AS STEEL STRIKERS FIGHT POLICE IN CHICAGO; MOB HALTED; MANY FELLED BY SHOTS
Four were killed and eighty-three persons went to hospitals with
gun-shot wounds, cracked heads, broken limbs or other injuries
received in a battle late this afternoon between police and steel
strikers at the gates of the Republic Steel Corporation plant in
South Chicago, Illinois.
*New York Times*

The meeting of strikers on May 30, acting on assurances by Mayor
Kelly that peaceful picketing was permissible, undertook to march
past the works of the Republic Steel Company as a gesture to the
workers within. The idea that they intended to attack the plant is
utterly preposterous. After parleying with the police and receiving a
few tear-gas bombs, the crowd was in retreat when the police began
firing. Following this, the police advanced, beating up the fugitives
with hatchet handles apparently furnished by the steel company. Ten
men were killed or died later from shots in the back or side. Those
unable to escape, including the wounded and dying, were thrown
helter-skelter into patrol wagons . . . Sixty-seven were arrested and
held unlawfully from Sunday evening until Thursday without being
booked. They are now awaiting trial according to the usual procedure
of the State's Attorney Courtney, who seems to have a habit of
covering up the misdoings of the police by prosecuting the victims.
*New Republic*; September 22, 1937

Labor does not seek industrial strife. It wants peace, but a peace with justice . . . The United States Chamber of Commerce, the National Association of Manufacturers and similar groups representing industry and financial interests, [are] encouraging a systematic organization of vigilante groups to fight unionization under the sham pretext of local interests. They equip these vigilantes with tin hats, wooden clubs, gas masks and lethal weapons and train them in the art of brutality and oppression. They bring in snoops, finks, hatchet gangs and Chowderhead Cohens to infest their plants and disturb the community . . .

No tin-hat brigade of goose-stepping vigilantes or bibble-babbling mob of blackguarding and corporation-paid scoundrels will prevent the onward march of labor.

John L. Lewis; September 3, 1937

Wallace Beery and Jean Harlow
in *Dinner at Eight*, 1933
Opposite: Busby Berkeley's
*Footlight Parade*, 1933

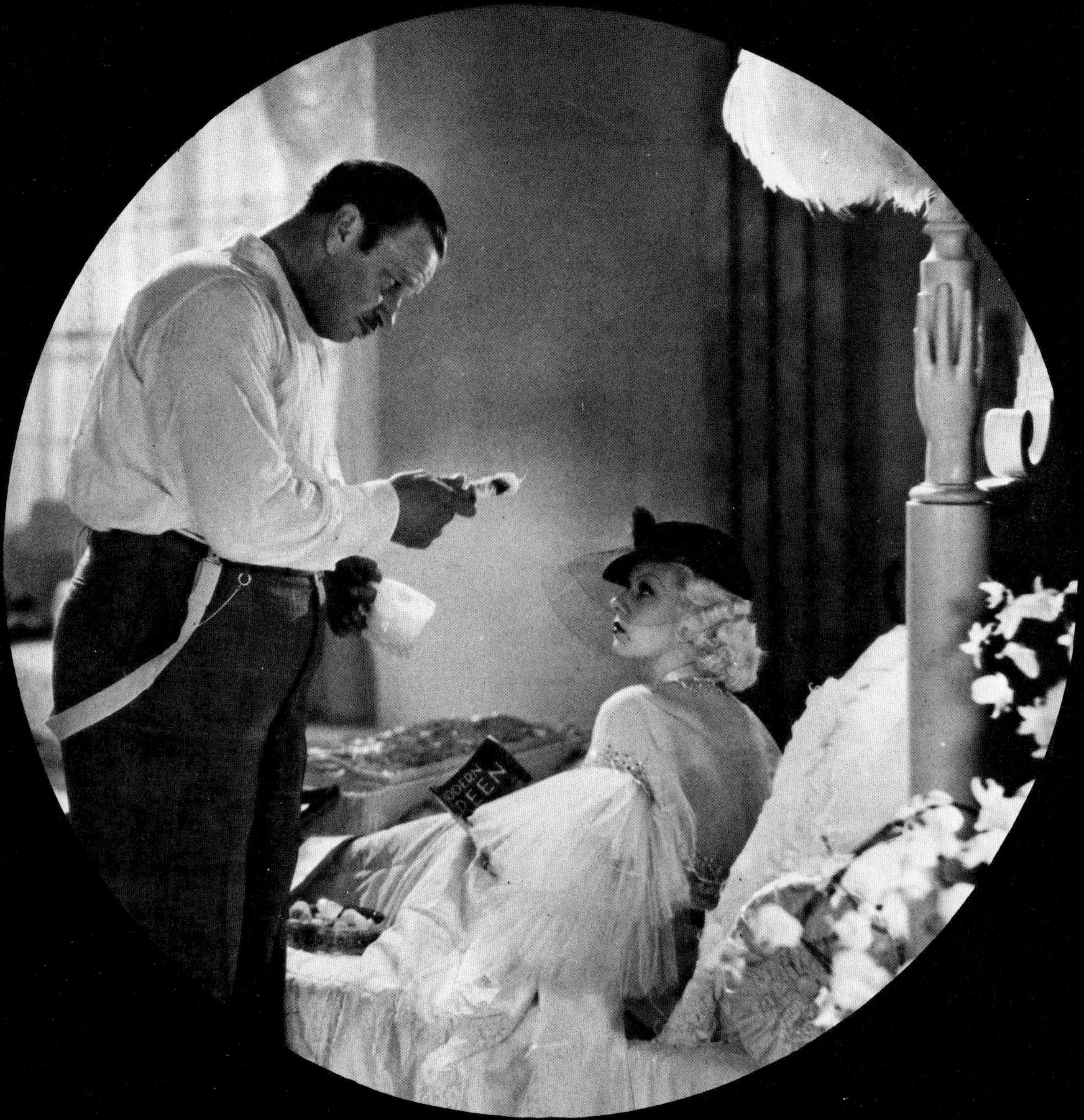

# HEAVEN ON STAGE EIGHT

## Einstein in Hollywood

*Warner Brothers have cabled Sigmund Freud, in London, asking him to come to Hollywood to assist the preparation of the new Bette Davis picture, Dark Victory.—News item*

Sigmund Freud had been in Hollywood about a year, and was engaged to marry Merle Oberon, when the studio got another great idea. Louella Parsons broke the story, and her papers gave it a two-column head:

WARNER BROS. TO FILM
THEORY OF RELATIVITY
Prof. Einstein Signed to Write Screen
Treatment of Own Story—Arrives
in Hollywood Next Month

Einstein's arrival in Hollywood, of course, was the signal for a gay round of dinners and cocktail parties. The Basil Rathbones, who had given a party in Freud's honor to which everyone came as his favorite neurosis, gave one for Einstein in which the guests were got up as their favorite numbers. Needless to say, there were some pretty hot numbers.

The climax, however, was a dinner at the Trocadero, given by the film colony as a whole, at which Will H. Hays was the principal speaker. 'The signing of Professor Einstein for pictures,' said Mr. Hays, 'is the greatest forward step that the industry has ever taken. American motion pictures appeal to people all over the world. I will be happy to okay Professor Einstein's contract just as soon as we get permission from Germany.'

Next morning, on the Warner lot, Professor Einstein was assigned an office in the writers' building and a stenographer named Goldie. Promptly at twelve o'clock he was summoned to a conference. The producer received him with a flourish.

'Professor,' he said, 'allow me to introduce Sol Bergen and Al Jenkins, who are going to work with you on the picture. Now, I've been thinking this thing over, and we want this to be absolutely *your* picture. What you say goes. But of course we all want a hit, and I'm sure you're willing to play ball with us. Now, I've got some great news for you. I've decided to put Joan Blondell in it.'

Sol Bergen let out a war whoop. 'Gee, Boss, that's great. Her name alone will put it over.'

'I want the Professor to have the best,' said the producer, 'because I'm sure he's going to give us a great picture. Now, Professor, here's the problem: how can we treat this theory of yours so as to keep it just as you wrote it—because this has got to be *your* picture—and still make it entertainment? Because first and foremost a motion picture has got to be entertainment. But of course we want your theory in it too.'

'I'm not sure that I've got the Professor's theory exactly straight,' said Al Jenkins. 'Would you mind, Professor, giving me just a quick summary of it, in a sort of non-technical way?'

'I don't think we have to bother the Professor about that,' said the producer. 'I've been thinking it over and I've got a great way to work it in. And here it is.' He leaned back and looked at them. 'The scene is a college where they *teach* this theory of the Professor's. Only it's a very *tough* theory, and there's never been a *girl* that's been able to understand it. Of course it's a co-ed college. And finally along comes a girl, attractive, of course, and says, "I am going to understand it."'

'Blondell!' said Sol Bergen.

'Right!' said the producer. 'So she pitches in and goes to work.

Cecil B. De Mille.
Below: Ruby Keeler in Busby
Berkeley's *Dames*, 1934

124

She won't go to parties or dances or anything, and she wears horn-rimmed glasses, and the boys think she's a grind and hasn't got any sex appeal. Underneath, of course, she's a regular girl.'

'There's got to be one guy in particular that falls for her,' said Jenkins.

'Sure!' said the producer, 'and I'll tell you who'd be great in the part. Wayne Morris. How's that, Professor? How'd you like to have Wayne Morris in your picture?'

'Let's make him the captain of the football team,' said Bergen. 'It'll give us a great finale.'

'Fine!' said the producer. 'Now, Blondell has got a girl friend that goes to college with her, only she's a different type. Flighty, and never does any studying, but a smart little kid when it comes to handling the boys. Knows 'em from A to Z. Now, there's a millionaire, an old grad that's just presented the college with a stadium, and his son is going to the college. Lots of money, and a racing car, and this little kid sets her cap for him. We could have a crack-up on the way back from the roadhouse.'

'Or else he could lead the college band,' said Bergen. 'That way you get your music in.'

'Great! And we have a kid playing the girl who can handle a couple of numbers. Here's an idea, Professor. How about Warren and Dubin for the score? How would you like that, huh?'

'And how's this?' asked Jenkins. 'She has another girl friend that sort of likes the older boys—with dough, see? And she sets out after the rich father.'

'I've got it!' said the producer. 'I've got the title! "Gold Diggers at College." Yes, sir, "Gold Diggers at College," by Albert Einstein, Sol Bergen, and Al Jenkins, based on the Theory of Relativity, by Albert Einstein. Professor, you've done a great picture!'
George S. Kaufman; *Nation*; August 6, 1938

I want mirrors and I want pillars. I have an idea for mirrors and pillars. And I want you to build heaven for me too, but we'll get to that later.
Busby Berkeley to studio technicians; 1934

## DE MILLE HUNTS GIRL FOR HIS NEXT FILM
Want to get into the movies? It's easy!

Cecil B. De Mille (with a big De, please) seeks a siren for the role of 'Anacaria,' a girl who crooned blues and danced a beguine for Nero, in Paramount's 'Sign of the Cross.' The part is right there awaiting any of you who wishes to be a star. There are a couple of requirements, of course, but nothing to worry over. All that Mr. De Mille desires is a girl possessing:

The flashing fiery eyes of Lenore Ulric;
The delicate, graceful hands of Pavlova;
The symmetrical legs of Marlene Dietrich;
The seductive voice of Josephine Baker;
The torso-tossing ability of Gilda Gray;
The mysterious allure of Greta Garbo.

Quite simple, you see. So step right up. The line forms to the right.

Incidentally, Mr. De Mille is ready to make all sacrifices for his art. In the most determined manner he declares:

'I'll find her if I have to sit through tests for the rest of the summer!'
*New York American*; August 12, 1932

125

## GRETA GARBO IS COMING BACK ...

And what's more—although this came from Hollywood and not from
La Garbo—her new salary is to be more than $11,000 a week, which
figures up to approximately $600,000 a year and is plenty of money in
any country, including the Scandinavian.

*Daily News*; July 27, 1932

Here are a couple of the latest told about town of the mysterious
Greta Garbo.

At a costume party where Greta was garbed as Hamlet a famous
feminine novelist and scenarist—name withheld—approached Garbo.

'How do you do, Miss Garbo?' said the novelist. 'I'm happy to
have this opportunity to meet you.'

Garbo drew back, pouted like a schoolgirl, and said:

'Go away. I don't want to know you.'

The novelist, thinking it was a gag, smiled and went on talking.

This time Garbo said harshly:

'I do not want to know you. Will you go away and let me alone?'

The novelist lost her temper and replied:

'Miss Garbo, you do not belong in a place like this—you are too
unsocial. The only excuse for giving any party is for the exchange of
social amenities; if you are not inclined to be sociable you should have
stayed at home.'

Folks who have met Garbo in her long walks say that if she is
addressed she will often make a face, scream at the speaker and run
away.

This is the other story: Garbo has a friend, a man who has been
associated with her in a business way for a long time. She will
occasionally pay calls at his home. His mother is a nice little old
gentlewoman who never goes to the movies and rarely reads the
newspapers, and hence is not conversant with the fact that somebody
named Greta Garbo is a celebrity.

One evening Garbo came home with her friend to supper—the
first time the man's mother had met Garbo. She received the star
graciously.

At supper the mother kept looking at Garbo, who was in a good
humor, and remarked:

'Have you ever tried getting into the movies, dear?'

Garbo was nonplussed for a moment but looking into the old lady's
gentle face she said softly: 'I've tried—.'

'Don't be discouraged, I think you might do well in pictures.'

*New York Sunday News*; July 10, 1932

I want a 'Hall of Mirrors,' an octagonal hall with walls entirely of
mirrors. Big mirrors. And a black floor that revolves. And a place in
the middle that stands still . . . Sixteen twenty foot mirrors around a
revolving floor . . . I'll be able to put a hundred girls in there and
they'll look like sixteen hundred.

Busby Berkeley; 1934

## The Making of a Movie Star

'Your complexion,' said the make-up man, 'is rich and rosy, and your
eyes are wide and full. Little eyes,' he mumbled, 'give me a pain.'

He squinted into my eyes. 'They're a good blue. That's okay.'

I was rather relieved. Everything seemed to be all right.

'Your hair line is good, too,' he said. 'No widow's peak. No wild
hair to be taken out.'

I breathed a sigh of relief. 'But,' he said, 'we'll have to pull out all your eyebrows! The line is bad.' . . .

'You'll have to have new teeth,' he said. One of my front teeth is a little short. To repair that and to straighten the line, he wanted most of my upper teeth taken out and replaced. Finally a dentist was able to make a shield that went over the short tooth, and that, they concluded, after six men stood around and made me smile at them for fifteen minutes, would be satisfactory.

'Your upper lip is too long,' said the make-up man. By this time I hated him as I never hated a man before. I wonder now that I didn't try to strangle him right there. He brought my nose closer to my mouth by broadening the mark of lipstick on my upper lip. 'And your face is lopsided. Your mouth droops on the right side and your jaw is lower on the right than the left.' So he raised the right corner of my mouth with lipstick and painted my right eyebrow line higher than the left, which raised the right side of my face.

Marlene Dietrich

I began to wonder why on earth they had employed me. With all this attention they could turn a scrubwoman into a lovely debutante, a cow-puncher into a Hamlet. Why didn't they go out and pick up a $10-a-day extra girl and save money?

I asked that question.

'Well,' they tried to explain, 'you see you have that—that, er—that Something that is difficult to find.' . . .

When they made the first test I sat in a chair with the camera pushed close to my face, and they moved lights and shouted to each other as though I were a horse. All day long the conversation went something like this: 'Hit her on the nose with that baby spot. No. Her nose won't stand it. Her chin's crooked. See if you can kill it. Try to burn down that upper lip.'

Then, with four or five men holding lights around me, the director said: 'Now we're all right Miss Sullavan. We'll shoot the test. Just be natural. Turn your head. That's it. Smile! SMILE! *Cut*! Stop everything. That smile, Miss Sullavan! It's terrible. We'll have to change it. Try again, and this time don't squint. Easy now. Just be natural.'

**The Making of a Movie Star**; Margaret Sullavan; *American Magazine*; May, 1934

Hooray for Hollywood; that gooey ballyhooley Hollywood,
Where any office boy or young mechanic
Can be a panic with just a good-looking pan.
Any shop girl can be a top girl,
If she pleases the tired businessman.

Hooray for Hollywood; you may be homely in your neighborhood.
Be an actor, see Mr. Factor, he'll make your kisser look good.
Go out and try your luck, you may be Donald Duck;
Hooray for Hollywood.

Hooray for Hollywood; they hire fellows whose physiques are good,
And then they tell them they're the perfect shape man
To act like ape man and convince them they should.
They make them shout and yell and people think they're swell
Oh! Hooray for Hollywood.
**Hooray for Hollywood**; song; Mercer and Whiting

I've got a swell idea about heaven. It'll take up all of Stage 8.
Busby Berkeley; 1934

## An All-Star Rebound to Normal
### Between Camera Shots of "Dinner at Eight"

*Metro-Goldwyn-Mayer's brilliant all-star production. Left to right: Standing—*EDMUND LOWE *(Dr. Talbot)*...GEORGE CUKOR, *Director*...LIONEL BARRYMORE *(Oliver Jordan)* JEAN HARLOW *(Kitty Packard)*...PHILLIPS HOLMES *(Ernest). Sitting—*MADGE EVANS *(Paula Jordan)*...LOUISE CLOSSER HALE *(Hattie Loomis)*...BILLIE BURKE *(Millicent Jordan)*...MARIE DRESSLER *(Carlotta Vance)* ...KAREN MORLEY *(Lucy Talbot)* ...GRANT MITCHELL *(Ed Loomis)*...A DAVID O. SELZNICK PRODUCTION.*

Drink
**Coca-Cola**
Delicious and Refreshing

In Hollywood, you see it every day in the making of pictures — *the pause that refreshes* with ice-cold Coca-Cola. It breaks the stress and strain of shooting scenes over and over. It is cooling relief from the hot kleig lights. It banishes drowsy yawns and hot, thirsty faces. It's the way to snap back to normal and be alert ... Because, an ice-cold Coca-Cola is more than just a drink. It combines those pleasant, wholesome substances which foremost scientists say do most to restore you to your normal self. Really delicious, it invites a pause, a pause that will refresh you.

Glamor doesn't make Frank [Capra]; Frank makes glamor (most of the ladies of the films would break a shapely leg to get into a picture of Capra's); and the shrewd heads of rival studios play close-to-the-bosom poker to get him . . . For he not only makes glamor; he makes pictures that make money. Not only is he rated in the councils of the moguls as worth at least half a million dollars a year to any studio that gets him—and don't let the press departments tell you *any* star makes that—but this spring he was officially marked as the ace of all directors when the Academy of Motion Picture Arts and Sciences awarded him, for 'It Happened One Night', the gold statuette for the biggest directorial achievement of the past year . . .

Capra is a picture-maker's picture-maker. And though the audience may give his name scant attention in the face of his actors' pretty antics, the picture-makers, and the picture-sellers in the theatres know his magic. The theatre owners know that the public goes to see a Capra picture whether they know it is a Capra picture or not. In other words, he has a recipe for pictures, a sort of signature, as is said about painters, whether their names are appended to the canvas or not . . .

Hollywood and its product being what they are, it is fair to say that the little wop is the most valued producer of entertainment in the world.

**Fine Italian Hand**; John Stuart; *Collier's*; August 17, 1935

Frank Capra and Gary Cooper.
Right: Shirley Temple

Suppose I'm not so cute when I grow up as I am now? . . . Suppose people don't want to see me in my pictures any more? Everybody at the studio says there's nothing to worry about. They keep saying that I'm not just an ordinary little girl who's learned to be just smart enough to do all that she's told. They say I've got 'natural talent,' like those little boys and girls who learn to play the piano and the violin at concerts long before they know how to read or write. I'll become a better actress as I get older, they say. People will always like me. They think I'll be good-looking, too. When Mom was 18 she looked like Norma Shearer, Daddy says. So mightn't I grow up to look just as nice?

But if I don't, and I'm forgotten, like all those other screen children who were once big stars—Daddy and Mom say that will be alright, too. Daddy says I'll soon be a rich girl. He's putting all the money I make in the bank for me. There'll be a good deal of it when I grow up, he says, even after he pays my income tax. Then I can go to college and get married. That's not such a bad idea, is it?
Shirley Temple; September, 1935

I curl [Shirley's hair] myself, to be sure it's done the simplest, safest way. I wouldn't like any artificial beauty methods used on a child. I just comb her hair with a little water, then brush each lock around my finger to curl it, and fasten each curl with a clasp pin so she can run and play while it sets and dries . . .

I do everything I can to have her grow up pretty, but I would never have her know it.
Shirley Temple's mother; May, 1936

**Bette Davis**

Give me sixty pianos. They must all be white—a dazzling white, to shine against a black background. They must be grand pianos—sixty of them!

And the pianos must dance! There'll be sixty girls sitting in front of them playing, and then the girls will dance and the pianos will dance with them!
Busby Berkeley; 1935

Much puzzlement has been in the Hollywood air lately because of the Gary Coopers' new habit of slipping into their car and tooling quietly away down the high-road—nearly always in the direction of Beverly Hills. Finally the mystery clears and is—a new house! . . .

The bedroom is carpeted to the baseboard in a rich soft cocoa color. Over this a two-level wheel rug of white. All walls are a marvellous dusty pink. Both these tones provide a perfect background for the luxurious bed, done from headboard to foot in off-white lapin. The chaise longue, in two parts, is richly tufted taffeta bound with beige French ribbon. The secretary, painted to represent tortoise shell, carries out the soft brown tone of the room. And a commode is of white lacquer decorated in brown. A six-panel mirror screen towers nine feet high, reflecting light and spaciousness from the six French windows. Before it is a glass boat mounted on a Louis XVI table with space beneath for books. White damask curtains hang in the doors, repeating the feeling of height from the screen . . .

All these warm tones, all this beauty of new materials and textures, all these chef-d'oeuvres from the looms and workshops of the world make up a house that is completely individual.
**A Movie Star's New Home**; *Arts & Decoration*; November, 1935

Too caustic? Well, if it's a good picture we'll make it. The hell with the cost.
Sam Goldwyn

### On the Trail of Pat Hobby
The day was dark from the outset, and a California fog crept everywhere. It had followed Pat in his headlong, hatless flight across the city. His destination, his refuge, was the studio, where he was not employed but which had been his home for twenty years.

Was it his imagination or did the policeman at the gate give him and his pass an especially long look? It might be the lack of a hat—Hollywood was full of hatless men but Pat felt marked, especially as there had been no opportunity to part his thin grey hair.

In the writers' building he went into the lavatory. Then he remembered: by some inspired ukase from above, all mirrors had been removed from the writers' building a year ago.

Across the hall he saw Bee McIlvaine's door ajar, and discerned her plump person.

'Bee, can you loan me your compact box?' he asked.

Bee looked at him suspiciously, then frowned and dug it from her purse.

'You on the lot?' she inquired.

'Will be next week,' he prophesied. He put the compact on her desk and bent over it with his comb. 'Why won't they put mirrors back in the johnnies? Do they think writers look at themselves all day?'

'Remember when they took out the couches?' said Bee. 'In nineteen thirty-two. And they put them back in in thirty-four.'

'I worked at home,' said Pat feelingly.

Finished with her mirror he wondered if she were good for a loan—enough to buy a hat and something to eat. Bee must have seen the look in his eyes for she forestalled him.

'The Finns got all my money,' she said, 'and I'm worried about my job. Either my picture starts tomorrow or it's going to be shelved. We haven't even got a title.'

She handed him a mimeographed bulletin from the scenario department and Pat glanced at the headline.

*To All Departments:*
*Title Wanted—Fifty Dollars Reward—Summary Follows*

'I could use fifty,' Pat said. 'What's it about?'

'It's written there. It's about a lot of stuff that goes on in tourist cabins.'

Pat started and looked at her wild-eyed. He had thought to be safe behind the guarded gates but news travelled fast. This was a friendly or perhaps not so friendly warning. He must move on. He was a hunted man now, with nowhere to lay his hatless head.

'I don't know anything about that,' he mumbled and walked hastily from the room.

## II

Just inside the door of the commissary Pat looked around. There was no guardian except the girl at the cigarette stand but obtaining another person's hat was subject to one complication: it was hard to judge the size by a cursory glance, while the sight of a man trying on several hats in a check room was unavoidably suspicious.

Personal taste also obtruded itself. Pat was beguiled by a green fedora with a sprightly feather but it was too readily identifiable. This was also true of a fine white Stetson for the open spaces. Finally he decided on a sturdy grey Homburg which looked as if it would give him good service. With trembling hands he put it on. It fitted. He walked out—in painful, interminable slow motion.

His confidence was partly restored in the next hour by the fact that no one he encountered made references to tourists' cabins. It had been a lean three months for Pat. He had regarded his job as a night clerk for the Selecto Tourist Cabins as a mere fill-in, never to be mentioned to his friends. But when the police squad came this morning they held up the raid long enough to assure Pat, or Don Smith as he called himself, that he would be wanted as a witness. The story of his escape lies in the realm of melodrama, how he went out a side door, bought a half pint of what he so desperately needed at the corner drugstore, hitch-hiked his way across the great city, going limp at the sight of traffic cops and only breathing free when he saw the studio's high-flown sign.

After a call on Louie, the studio bookie, whose great patron he had once been, he dropped in on Jack Berners. He had no idea to submit, but he caught Jack in a hurried moment flying off to a producers' conference and was unexpectedly invited to step in and wait for his return.

The office was rich and comfortable. There were no letters worth reading on the desk, but there were a decanter and glasses in a cupboard and presently he lay down on a big soft couch and fell asleep.

He was awakened by Berners' return, in high indignation.

'Of all the damn nonsense! We get a hurry call—heads of all departments. One man is late and we wait for him. He comes in and gets a bawling out for wasting thousands of dollars worth of time. Then what do you suppose: Mr. Marcus has lost his favorite hat!'

Pat failed to associate the hat with himself.

Ginger Rogers off and on set
(in *Top Hat*, 1935)

'All the department heads stop production!' continued Berners. 'Two thousand people look for a grey Homburg hat!' He sank despairingly into a chair. 'I can't talk to you today, Pat. By four o'clock, I've got to get a title to a picture about a tourist camp. Got an idea?'

'No,' said Pat. 'No.'

'Well, go up to Bee McIlvaine's office and help her figure something out. There's fifty dollars in it.'

In a daze Pat wandered to the door.

'Hey,' said Berners, 'don't forget your hat.'

### III

Feeling the effects of his day outside the law, and of a tumbler full of Berners' brandy, Pat sat in Bee McIlvaine's office.

'We've got to get a title,' said Bee gloomily.

She handed Pat the mimeograph offering fifty dollars reward and put a pencil in his hand. Pat stared at the paper unseeingly.

'How about it?' she asked. 'Who's got a title?'

There was a long silence.

'*Test Pilot*'s been used, hasn't it?' he said with a vague tone.

'Wake up! This isn't about aviation.'

'Well, I was just thinking it was a good title.'

'So's *Birth of a Nation*.'

'But not for this picture,' Pat muttered. '*Birth of a Nation* wouldn't suit this picture.'

'Are you ribbing me?' demanded Bee. 'Or are you losing your mind? This is serious.'

'Sure—I know.' Feebly he scrawled words at the bottom of the page. 'I've had a couple of drinks that's all. My head'll clear up in a minute. I'm trying to think what have been the most successful titles. The trouble is they've all been used, like *It Happened One Night*.'

Bee looked at him uneasily. He was having trouble keeping his eyes open and she did not want him to pass out in her office. After a minute she called Jack Berners.

'Could you possibly come up? I've got some title ideas.'

Jack arrived with a sheaf of suggestions sent in from here and there in the studio, but digging through them yielded no ore.

'How about it, Pat? Got anything?'

Pat braced himself to an effort.

'I like *It Happened One Morning*,' he said—and then looked desperately at his scrawl on the mimeograph paper, 'or else—*Grand Motel*.'

Berners smiled.

'*Grand Motel*,' he repeated. 'By God! I think you've got something. *Grand Motel*.'

'I said *Grand Hotel*,' said Pat.

'No, you didn't. You said *Grand Motel*—and for my money it wins the fifty.'

'I've got to lie down,' announced Pat. 'I feel sick.'

'There's an empty office across the way. That's a funny idea Pat, *Grand Motel*—or else *Motel Clerk*. How do you like that?'

As the fugitive quickened his step out the door Bee pressed the hat into his hands.

'Good work, old timer,' she said.

Pat seized Mr. Marcus' hat, and stood holding it there like a bowl of soup.

'Feel—better—now,' he mumbled after a moment. 'Be back for the money.'

And carrying his burden he shambled toward the lavatory.

**On the Trail of Pat Hobby**; F. Scott Fitzgerald; *Esquire*; January, 1941

**Carole Lombard and George Raft**

## THIS YEAR'S LOVE MARKET

**October, 1937** Marriage held firm, in spite of bearish interest in the Clark Gable menage, with rumored participation by Carole Lombard . . . Rumors of a rise in Garbo-Stokowski, formerly unlisted, were denied by the company involved.

**November** Public participation was marked. Traders and usually authoritative sources rumored new listings and the gossip tape lagged behind events. The new Tyrone Power consolidation mentioned Janet Gaynor. The Ginger Rogers-Playwright Robert Riskin deal attracted attention. Carole Lombard and Clark Gable were bracketed for a sharp rally.

**December** Early in the month several matrimonial issues were retired: Leopold Stokowski changed his listing and tape symbol from Husband to Divorcee . . . There was profit-taking in Stork Preferred by Henry Fonda and wife . . . A broadly bullish tone prevailed, with Cary Grant-Phyllis Brooks and Loretta Young-Joe Mankiewicz moving briskly.

**July, 1938** Romances shared in the month's recovery, along with Matrimonial shares, on a broad front. Hepburn stock broke through the old high, with rumored association with Howard Hughes.

**August** Marriages rebounded when Humphrey Bogart, twice divorced, and Mayo Methot, once divorced, were merged in a new corporation . . .

**September** A setback was caused by a hinted Reno visit by Bette Davis. The Tyrone Power issue, which had been very volatile until recent months, again rallied sharply with much widespread participation. The Norma Shearer firm was rumored to have the largest commitments in T.P. Preferred.
*Photoplay*; January, 1939

I have known of Hollywood love affairs, not as the gossip twists them, but rather as beautiful romances while they lasted. I believe that love is one of the main reasons for existing . . .

Hollywood has been called 'heartbreak town' by a number of sentimental writers. Well, maybe it is, but it's a swell place after all.

Oh yes, and I've also written a book revealing all my eighteen years in Hollywood. You see, I know what a young girl doesn't know!
Betty Compson

Man is born with a dominant ego—offend that ego or compete with it in the same field and, if you are a woman, you will soon be a divorcee.
Clark Gable

Fundamentally, screen kisses are divided into three parts. The approach to the kiss is the first part. The kiss proper (or improper) is the second part. The retreat from the kiss is the third—and usually, the most difficult part.

The kiss itself must always be left to the instincts and caprices of the kissers themselves. The director has to be sure that the man's nose doesn't hide the girl's eyes and that neither face is distorted by the camera angle. But the kiss itself can only be regulated by the kisser and the kissed—just as in real life.
Busby Berkeley; 1938

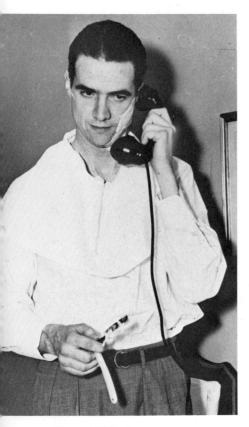

**Howard Hughes**

January 14, 1936
## MOVIE PRODUCER CUTS AIR TIME FROM COAST; HOWARD HUGHES REACHES NEW YORK FROM LOS ANGELES IN 9 HRS. 27 MINS.
'I wanted to see New York,' he said, 'so I tried to see how fast I could do it in.'
*New York Times*

May 15, 1936
## HUGHES SETS MARK, SPENDS $500 TO WIN $50
Howard Hughes won a $50 bet tonight, but he spent $500 to do it. Hughes had luncheon in Chicago and dinner in Glendale, California, just as he wagered he would.
*New York Daily News*

The trouble with this business is the dearth of bad pictures.
Sam Goldwyn

## CELLULOID RAINBOW FOR HOLLYWOOD
Last week in his paneled Hollywood office, Goldwyn addressed subordinates:
'All Goldwyn pictures will henceforth be done in color.'
Since Goldwyn is dean of Hollywood's producers, its largest individual producer and owner of Samuel Goldwyn, Inc., a $5,000,000 corporation, his statement astounded the movie industry.
Yet, though Goldwyn's decision even might mean the death knell for black-and-white pictures, movie folk failed to don mourning. Lots buzzed with gossip about the significance of the decision, but production of black-and-white films continued briskly. Cameras churned and directors bawled orders . . .
In his first three color pictures Goldwyn will glorify Goldwyn in the 'Goldwyn Follies,' starring Helen Jepson, Metropolitan Opera diva. He will spend about $2,000,000 on this 'supermusical.' Of this, some $600,000 has been allocated to color costs. Production starts August 1 . . .
Another possibility this year is 'Gone With the Wind.' Selznick–International has bought the screen rights. Moviegoers lifted curious eyebrows recently on reading that Mrs. Jock Whitney had been tested as a prospect for the coveted role of Scarlett O'Hara . . . Should Mrs. Whitney get the role she would be a dark horse winner in a race in which almost every possible Hollywood actress has been entered by fans.
*Literary Digest*; May, 1937

Orson Welles officially has become part of Hollywood. He has rented the Mary Pickford–Buddy Rogers manse; he dictates while floating in his swimming pool; he visits the studio in soiled dungarees and an ancient sweatshirt; he has held animated and noisy story conferences in the Brown Derby's Bamboo Room; he is a neighbor of Garbo, Bette Davis and Shirley Temple and, best of all, he has been received by Miss Temple, has ridden on her merry-go-round and has been photographed with her. Because of these achievements, he has been accepted by Hollywood, in spite of the fact that he was looked upon on his arrival with open suspicion because of his beard.
*New York Times*; August 20, 1939

December 18, 1939

## ATLANTA PREMIERE OF 'GONE WITH THE WIND' STIRS SOUTH TO TEARS & CHEERS

### SELZNICK COMPLETES SIEGE OF ATLANTA

'Gone With the Wind' has what it wanted most—the unrestrained approval of the deep South.

Hollywood didn't matter. The Middle West doesn't matter. Even tomorrow's spectacular first night at the Astor and Capitol doesn't matter. For the South has accepted 'Gone With the Wind' and that was what Producer David O. Selznick had prayed for most eloquently . . .

Atlanta had said yes to his long, long effort. Atlanta had agreed that he had done right by their favorite daughter, Margaret Mitchell. Even the smallest detail had been found authentic.

Accent? Well, in the first place there isn't a great deal of accent in the film. But what there is never becomes pronounced or ostentatious. It is never more than the cultured, well-bred Southern speech.

Atmosphere? The scenes are as real as if they'd been taken on the red earth of Georgia. Technicolor was never more eloquent than it is in this picture. It is a long way from 'Becky Sharp' or 'Ramona' to 'Gone With the Wind.'

Scarlett O'Hara? In true life Vivien Leigh is a quiet, pretty little woman without any great apparent power of attraction. But in this film her green eyes flash with violent moods, clashing passions and the soft longing for love that characterized Scarlett, whose life was a constant warfare between the inherited fire of her father and the peace of her mother. Miss Leigh is the Scarlett you've always had in mind.

Rhett Butler? Clark Gable is Rhett, of course. He swept Atlanta off its feet both on the screen and in person. It is a good thing he took his wife, Carole Lombard, with him!

The war scenes? The burning of Atlanta? These brought some subdued hisses on the part of old veterans in the audience, and it was suspected that several of them wanted to march up the aisle and take another crack at Sherman. But no one questioned the scenic authenticity . . .

Tomorrow night one expects great doings on Broadway at the double premiere. But as far as Selznick is concerned it's all over—Atlanta has been captured.

*New York World Telegram*; December 18, 1939

December 20, 1939

## 'GONE WITH THE WIND' ARRIVES; NEW YORK GOES MILDLY AND PLEASANTLY MAD

The New York Film Critics Circle rejected the anti-democratic, anti-Negro film, 'Gone With the Wind,' and voted 'Wuthering Heights' the best Hollywood film of the year Tuesday night . . .

It took the critics $2\frac{1}{2}$ hours and 14 ballots to eliminate one of the most disgraceful films ever produced in Hollywood. The final ballot stood 13 for 'Wuthering Heights,' 3 for 'Gone With the Wind,' and one for 'Ninotchka.'

*Daily Worker*; December 28, 1939

April 24, 1940

## 'GONE WITH THE WIND' PASSES $17,000,000; EXPECTED TO GROSS 30 MILLION IN U.S.

## A STORY OF TWO MUSTACHES

Among the worries of Adolph Hitler—for thus bizarre, sometimes, are the inside facts of world history—is another little man with a funny mustache. The second little man does not really exist. He is the tragicomic figure created by Charlie Chaplin so many years ago; a thing of lights and shadows merely.

Yet it may be stated as a fact that Hitler, if he can devise some way to do so, will have a print of Chaplin's forthcoming film, now called

'The Dictator,' smuggled to his mountain retreat at Berchtesgaden. It might be smart for the Allies to let him, for Hitler's rage and chagrin on viewing the picture will be extreme. Changes are still possible, but unless radical ones are made Chaplin will first be seen as a Jewish barber wearing the baggy pants and derby hat of old, carrying his cane—with the silly mustache on his lip. Through some fantastic mistake he is then mistaken for Hitler and becomes a fearsome, roaring, screaming Fuehrer. But the same silly mustache is on his lip.

By midsummer of this year 'The Dictator' will be shown throughout the world—except in the German Reich, obviously—and hundreds of thousands of people will be roaring with laughter at Chaplin's portrayal of Hitler. And the head of the German Reich is very well aware that danger lies in being laughed at.

Henry Pringle; *Ladies' Home Journal*; July, 1940

Now that the waiting is over and the shivers of suspense at an end, let the trumpets be sounded and banners flung against the sky. For the little tramp, Charlie Chaplin, finally emerged last night from behind the close-guarded curtains which have concealed his activities these past two years and presented himself in triumphal splendor as 'The Great Dictator'—or you know who.

No event in the history of the screen has ever been anticipated with more hopeful excitement than the premiere of this film; . . . no picture ever made has promised more momentous consequences. The prospect of little 'Charlot,' the most universally loved character in the world, directing his superlative talent for ridicule against the most dangerously evil man alive has loomed as a titanic jest, a transcendent paradox. And the happy report this morning is that it comes off magnificently. 'The Great Dictator' may not be the finest picture ever made—in fact, it possesses several disappointing shortcomings. But, despite them, it turns out to be a truly superb accomplishment by a truly great artist—and, from one point of view, perhaps the most significant film ever produced.

Bosley Crowther; *New York Times*; October 16, 1940

Charlie Chaplin in *The Great Dictator*, **1940**

## ORSON'S $1,000,000 GAMBLE

Orson Welles makes a picture called 'Citizen Kane' that allegedly parallels the life story of a prominent man still among the living. Amazingly, no one at Welles' studio knows anything about the movie's contents until it is off the sound stages and ready for release.

A hubbub is raised. Legal threats are made; the picture must not be shown in its present form. The studio goes right on making it ready for distribution. If the film is tossed on the shelf, $1,200,000 goes up in smoke.

That's a poser, all right, but to us the most fantastic phase of the squabble is this:

How could a major motion picture studio hand over more than a million dollars to a young untried producer without knowing exactly what kind of story he was going to make?

Apparently the company didn't know. From inquiries around the RKO lot yesterday we gathered that no one except Welles and his own particular little acting group brought out from the East, had the slightest knowledge of what was being filmed by RKO's cameras . . .

Regardless of grounds or lack of grounds for the complainant's grievance, the fact stands out that poor old Hollywood once more has been 'taken in'—this time in a manner more ludicrous than ever before.

Harold Heffernan; *Chicago Daily News*; January 17, 1941

## HEARST OVER HOLLYWOOD

Will Hollywood stand up to William Randolph Hearst over the matter of Orson Welles' film 'Citizen Kane'? RKO, the distributor, announces that it is going ahead with plans to show the picture. It has been booked into the number-one movie house of the nation, the Radio City Music Hall in New York City, and many other places. But the films are so notoriously timid when confronted by the power of a journalistic overlord like Hearst that many people find it hard to believe the producers really intend to defy the lord of San Simeon.

Hollywood trembled when the first threats came that the Hearst newspapers would open an editorial attack upon the motion-picture industry unless the film was censored or suppressed. Underlings of the aged publisher made the threat after seeing the picture. Nothing was put into writing, but *Variety*, on January 15, reported that 'steady bombardment from the heaviest artillery in the Hearst press is faced by the entire film industry as a result of the fury into which William Randolph Hearst has been thrown by the revelation that the story of "Citizen Kane," Orson Welles' first film, bears similarity to the life of the publisher' . . .

Orson Welles wrote the script of 'Citizen Kane,' played the leading role, directed and produced the picture. The story deals with a young heir to a fortune in mining stock who comes to New York from the West, launches a gaudy newspaper, campaigns for the governorship of New York and editorializes vigorously for war with Spain in Cuba. He attempts to promote the fortunes of a pretty blonde opera singer and fires his best writer for doing a concert review that showed the lady's singular lack of talent. At the end, embittered and unlamented, he dies amid the splendors of a great Florida castle he stuffed with antiques and art treasures.

Charles Kane differs from William Randolph Hearst in many ways. For one thing, he is a sympathetic character.

Michael Sage; *Nation*; February 24, 1941

Within the withering spotlight as no other film has ever been before, Orson Welles' 'Citizen Kane' had its world premiere at the Palace last evening. And now that the wraps are off, the mystery has been exposed and Mr. Welles and the RKO directors have taken the much-debated leap, it can be safely stated that the suppression of this film would have been a crime. For, in spite of some disconcerting lapses and strange ambiguities in the creation of the principal character, 'Citizen Kane' is far and away the most surprising and cinematically exciting picture to be seen here in many a moon. As a matter of fact, it comes close to being the most sensational film ever made in Hollywood.
Bosley Crowther; *New York Times*; May 2, 1941

BROTHER, CAN YOU SPARE A BILLION?

The *Hindenburg* over New York
en route to Lakehurst, N.J., 1937

We know now that in the early years of the twentieth century this world was being watched closely by intelligences greater than man's and yet as mortal as his own. We know now that as human beings busied themselves about their various concerns they were scrutinized and studied, perhaps almost as narrowly as a man with a microscope might scrutinize the transient creatures that swarm and multiply in a drop of water. With infinite complacence people went to and fro over the earth about their little affairs, serene in the assurance of their dominion over this small spinning fragment of solar driftwood which by chance or design man has inherited out of the dark mystery of Time and Space. Yet across an immense ethereal gulf, minds that are to our minds as ours are to the beasts in the jungle, intellects vast, cool and unsympathetic, regarded this earth with envious eyes and slowly and surely drew their plans against us. In the thirty-eighth year of the twentieth century came the great disillusionment.

**Invasion from Mars**; Howard Koch; *Columbia Broadcasting System*;
October 30, 1938

October 1, 1938

## BRITAIN & GERMANY MAKE ANTI-WAR PACT; HITLER & CHAMBERLAIN VOICE THEIR NATIONS WILL NEVER FIGHT; DEMOBILIZATION FORESEEN

Ever since a storm began revolving about the head of Colonel Charles A. Lindbergh—over whether or not, during the Czech crisis, he told a group of influential Britons that the Nazi airforce was stronger than all the rest of Europe's combined, he has been in Germany touring aircraft plants. Last week, since the flyer was still in Berlin, American Ambassador Hugh R. Wilson decided to honor him with a stag dinner. To it the envoy invited Field Marshal Hermann Goering, assorted Nazi notables, and several foreign diplomats.

When Goering arrived he went up to Lindbergh, produced a small box, and proclaimed: 'in the name of the Fuhrer—!' Then the No. 2 Nazi hung the Service Cross of the Order of the German Eagle around Lindbergh's neck and pinned on his chest the six-pointed star that goes with it. The American seemed surprised but glowed with embarrassed pride and wore the decoration the rest of the evening.
*Newsweek*; October 31, 1938

Hitler has shown the whole world a new idea in government—a good idea. We, as American-Germans, must stand with him like they are doing in Germany.
Fritz Kuhn; German-American Bund; 1939

The fiery cross of the Klan brought terror to those who had cause to fear . . . the burning of the swastika will have the same effect on the Reds and their sympathizers, including the Jews, as it had on the Negro and the carpetbagger . . . You are urged to cooperate in covering the nation with the fiery swastika, for the enemy is extremely jittery.
George E. Deatherage; Knights of the White Camelia; 1939

A war which threatened to envelop the world in flames has been averted: but it has become increasingly clear that world peace is not assured.

We have learned that long before any overt military act, aggression begins with the preliminaries of propaganda, subsidized penetration, the loosening of ties of good will, the stirring of prejudice and the incitement to disunion . . .

The deadline of danger from within and without is not within our control.
Franklin D. Roosevelt; January 4, 1939

February 21, 1939

## 22,000 NAZIS HOLD RALLY IN MADISON SQUARE GARDEN

Only the German-American Bund, which was sponsoring it, didn't call it a rally. They called it 'George Washington's Birthday Exercises.' But that didn't fool anybody—least of all the Bund members themselves, though they put on a good front . . .

[Inside] there is a huge flood-lighted platform, and from the back of it a panel bearing a picture of George Washington rises half-way to the ceiling. It is flanked by other panels, painted red, with nazi insignia upon which the United States coat of arms has been imposed. On either side of the hockey scoreboards and clocks on the balcony

there are enormous slogans in red and black: 'Wake up America'; 'Smash Jewish Communism'; 'Stop Jewish Domination of Christian America'; 'One Million Bund Members by 1940.' Somehow they seem hideously incongruous there beside the hockey and baseball ads.

Everything is marvellously efficient. The meeting begins on time! An orchestra in full dress plays patriotic and operatic airs. Five minutes before eight a boys' drum and bugle corps in brown shirts and light brown trousers marches up on the platform. Their leader shouts a sharp command. They begin to play. Then from the back of the Garden somewhere the Bund begins marching toward the platform. First the color-bearers, with the small red and gold swastika standard in front, then the American flags, the Italian flag, the German banners and the emblems of the German-American Bund. They mass the colors behind the speakers' dais on the platform, beneath the picture of George Washington.

After the flags come the storm troopers, hundreds of them, in grey shirts with Sam Browne belts, black trousers and black overseas caps. They wear neat black ties, fastened with gold swastika stick-pins. They come down first one aisle, then another, and another, and they keep coming from somewhere, marching stiffly erect; it seems as though they will never stop coming. The crowd rises and extends arms in the nazi salute. From somewhere aloft a soft blue spotlight plays on the marching men. The crowd is almost carried away. It is all here—the massed flags, the stirring music, the slogans, the spotlight, the imminent hysteria.

I Went to a Nazi Rally; Alson J. Smith; *Christian Century*; March 8, 1939

I saw in New York the same scenes I witnessed in Berlin seven years ago.
Dorothy Thompson; February, 1939

March 16, 1939

## GERMAN TROOPS MARCH INTO CZECHOSLOVAKIA IN DEFIANCE OF TREATY; CRISIS VERY GRAVE AS WORLD WAITS

To have peace and prosperity forever, each nation must kill its own Jews. When the last hour for the Jew in America strikes, there will be no passover. Jews, America is your last mile!
American Gentile Youth Movement; sticker; 1939

One of the ominous distinctions of American Fascism is that, without benefit of a Mussolini, a Hitler or even an Oswald Mosley, it continues to prosper and spread. The source of the prosperity is something of a mystery. But of the spread there can be no doubt . . .

There is no important strain in this country of the older and milder Fascism of Mussolini. America's Fascists are the ideological offspring of Hitler and National Socialism. Some of them frankly acknowledge it. Many of them admit only to an affinity. Most of them deny that they aim for the Nazi state. But in all of them, regardless of how much or how little they concede, the Nazi family features are too plain to be missed . . .

For fuel for their movement the Nazis mixed patriotism with hate. Their American kinsmen use the same mixture. They hate the same things, in the same order and for the same reasons. They hate the Communists for whatever reasons seem, at the moment, most likely to catch on. They hate the Jews because Communism and sundry

Left: German-American Bund rally, New York City, 1939. Below: Camp Siegfried, New Jersey

## WAKE UP AMERICANS!
## DO YOU WANT THIS?

Clean up America! Break the Red Plague!
## BOYCOTT the JEW!

other evils must have some visible incarnation and the Jews are handy and outnumbered. On behalf of the Founding Fathers, they hate democracy. The Founding Fathers, they maintain, did not found a democracy—'mob rule'—but a republic—'a government of representatives.' They hate the New Deal exactly and no less venomously than the Nazis hated the German republic, because it appears, to them, to have given the form and substance to all the other things they hate . . . In support and for the spread of these hatreds, they are pouring on the country an extensive propaganda which, for incoherent violence, might be drawn directly from the presses of Joseph Geobbels or Julius Streicher—and some of it actually is.

**Star-Spangled Fascists**; Stanley High; *Saturday Evening Post*; May 27, 1939

Youth, Youth—We are the future soldiers.
Youth, Youth—We are the ones to carry out future deeds.
Yes; by our fists will be smashed whoever stands in our way.
Youth, Youth—We are the future soldiers.
Youth, Youth—We are the ones to carry out future deeds.
Fuhrer—We belong to you; yes, we comrades belong to you.
German–American Bund youth camp song; 1938

148

# 2022
# STANDARD POSTAGE
# STAMP CATALOGUE

ONE HUNDRED AND SEVENTY-EIGHTH EDITION IN SIX VOLUMES

## Volume 1A

### U.S., U.N., A-Australia

| | |
|---|---|
| EDITOR-IN-CHIEF | Jay Bigalke |
| EDITOR-AT-LARGE | Donna Houseman |
| CONTRIBUTING EDITOR | Charles Snee |
| EDITOR EMERITUS | James E. Kloetzel |
| SENIOR EDITOR /NEW ISSUES AND VALUING | Martin J. Frankevicz |
| ADMINISTRATIVE ASSISTANT/CATALOGUE LAYOUT | Eric Wiessinger |
| PRINTING AND IMAGE COORDINATOR | Stacey Mahan |
| SENIOR GRAPHIC DESIGNER | Cinda McAlexander |
| SALES DIRECTOR | David Pistello |
| SALES DIRECTOR | Eric Roth |

Released April 2021
Includes New Stamp Listings through the February 2021 Linn's Stamp News Monthly Catalogue Update

Copyright© 2021 by

# AMOS MEDIA

1660 Campbell Road, Suite A, Sidney, OH 45365
Publishers of *Linn's Stamp News, Linn's Stamp News Monthly, Coin World* and *Coin World Monthly*.

## SELLING GEORGE VI TO THE U.S.
Selling a King and Queen of England to the United States is essentially a public-relations job, just as much as it would be to sell a product made in Great Britain, and for the purposes of this memorandum we can consider that the product to be sold to the United States is 'good will.' . . .

It is obvious to America that the step of sending George VI and Queen Elizabeth to America was not taken without long consideration of the profits to be derived from such a move. Even though the American part of the trip is supposed to be a side excursion from the royal visit to Canada, it does not detract from the fact that in the eyes of the world, and of America in particular, the few days the King and Queen will spend on American soil and in contact with Americans will be the most potentially important part of the entire trip so far as the future of British Empire good will in this hemisphere is concerned.

Josef Israels; *Scribner's*; February, 1939

June 8, 1939
## HULL EXTENDS NATION'S HAND IN WELCOME TO ROYALTY AT BORDER; KING SPEEDS TO MEET FDR
When the King and Queen crossed a narrow strip of carpet in the middle of Suspension Bridge [Niagara Falls] last night, a thousand typewriters began pounding that history had just been made.
*New York Times*

June 9, 1939
## KING & QUEEN GUESTS AT THE WHITE HOUSE; GEORGE HOPES WE WILL EVER WALK IN FRIENDSHIP

June 10, 1939
## CROWDS LINE ROUTE; THRONGS WAIT HOURS & THEN ROAR GREETINGS AS SOVEREIGNS PASS

June 12, 1939
## KING, QUEEN BID U.S. FAREWELL, THANKS FOR THE HOT DOGS!

September 1, 1939
## GERMAN PLANES BOMB HEART OF WARSAW: LONDON, PARIS GIVE REICH LAST WARNING

September 3, 1939
## BRITAIN AND FRANCE AT WAR

Tonight my single duty is to speak to the whole of America.

Until four-thirty this morning I had hoped against hope that some miracle would prevent a devastating war in Europe and bring to an end the invasion of Poland by Germany.

For four long years a succession of actual wars and constant crises have shaken the entire world and have threatened in each case to bring on the gigantic conflict which is today unhappily a fact . . .

It is easy for you and for me to shrug our shoulders and to say that conflicts taking place thousands of miles from the continental United States, and, indeed, thousands of miles from the whole American Hemisphere, do not seriously affect the Americas—and that all the United States has to do is to ignore them and go about its own

business. Passionately though we may desire detachment, we are forced to realize that every word that comes through the air, every ship that sails the sea, every battle that is fought does affect the American future . . .

This nation will remain a neutral nation but I cannot ask that every American remain neutral in thought as well. Even a neutral has a right to take account of facts. Even a neutral cannot be asked to close his mind or close his conscience.

I have said not once but many times that I have seen war and that I hate war. I say that again and again.

I hope the United States will keep out of this war. I believe that it will. And I give you assurance and reassurance that every effort of your government will be directed toward that end.

As long as it remains within my power to prevent, there will be no blackout of peace in the United States.

Franklin D. Roosevelt; September 3, 1939

I am more confirmed than ever in my belief that not a dollar should be wasted nor a drop of American blood nor a single American soldier should be sacrificed over the boundary disputes of the Old World.

Senator Ludden; 1939

September 16, 1939

## LINDBERGH URGES WE SHUN WAR

I speak tonight to those people in the United States of America who feel that the destiny of this country does not call for our involvement in European wars . . .

Charles Lindbergh speaking and (inset) with Senator Burton K. Wheeler, at America First Committee rallies

These wars in Europe are not wars in which our civilization is defending itself against some Asiatic intruder. There is no Genghis Khan or Xerxes marching against our Western nations. This is not a question of banding together to defend the white race against foreign invasion. This is simply one more of those age-old struggles within our own family of nations—a quarrel arising from the errors of the last war—from the failure of the victors of that war to follow a consistent policy of either fairness or force . . .

We must not be misguided by foreign propaganda to the effect that our frontiers lie in Europe. One need only glance at a map to see where our true frontiers lie. What more could we ask than the Atlantic Ocean on the East and the Pacific on the West? No, our interests in Europe need not be from the standpoint of defense. Our own natural frontiers are enough for that. If we extend them at all, we might as well extend them around the earth. An ocean is a formidable barrier, even for modern aircraft.
Charles Lindbergh; September 15, 1939

I am hoping for my country for the avoidance of the cost, the waste, the debt, the futility, the deaths, the heartbreak and the cripples that can be our only American reward for engagement in another terrible European mess.
Senator Gerald Nye; September, 1939

Keep American boys and America itself out of Europe's wars over boundary lines and struggles for power.
Senator Capper; 1939

Say, those guys are crazy. Hitler—pffff! Why can't they get together and talk things over? They're all crazy over there. There's no need of war, and there's no need for America to get mixed up in another one. Peace is what we want. All this shooting and killing is the bunk.
Al Capone; October, 1939

Things move with such terrific speed these days that it really is essential to us to think in broader terms and, in effect, to warn the American people that they, too, should think of possible ultimate results in Europe . . . Therefore, my sage old friend, my problem is to get the American people to think of conceivable consequences without scaring the American people into thinking that they are going to be dragged into the war.
Franklin D. Roosevelt; letter to William Allen White; December, 1939

May 10, 1940
## NAZIS INVADE HOLLAND, BELGIUM, LUXEMBOURG BY LAND AND AIR

May 17, 1940
## ROOSEVELT ASKS BILLION FOR DEFENSE

June 6, 1940
## NAZIS ATTACK FRENCH ON 120-MILE FRONT
In the past we have dealt with a Europe dominated by England and France. In the future we may have to deal with a Europe dominated by Germany.
Charles Lindbergh; August, 1940

## WENDELL WILLKIE FOR PRESIDENT!
Help Oren Root jr. organize the people's demand for Willkie. Send Root a contribution to 15 Broad St., New York.
Public notice; *New York Herald Tribune*; winter, 1940

For the last month or so our desk has been cluttered with petitions, reprints of editorials, letters, and one thing and another from Mr. Oren Root, Jr., who wants everybody to help him put Wendell Willkie in the White House. 'If we elect him President,' one of the letters stated, 'we will see the dawn of a New World.' With those words ringing in our head, we called on Mr. Root last week and asked him what he meant. 'Gosh,' he said, 'I have no idea.' He explained that they were dashed off in a white heat right after his first meeting with Mr. Willkie, whose 'colossal charm' had so affected him that he just let himself go . . .

The idea of sending Mr. Willkie from Wall Street to Pennsylvania Avenue, a distance regarded by practical politicians as about equivalent to that between King Arthur's Round Table and the Holy Grail, germinated in Mr. Root's mind sometime last winter . . .

The Root machine has now collected Willkie petitions from every state and territory. They have been arriving at Mr. Root's apartment at the rate of about five hundred a week. After they've been sorted by Mr. Root (assisted by the maid), they are stacked in packing cases and carted off to the basement storeroom. So far Mr. Root has laid down four cases and one barrel of petitions. These, augmented, will be taken to the convention. He expects to have 250,000 signatures by then, a number he thinks will not be lightly laughed off. 'The movement,' he said excitedly as we were leaving, 'is taking on the force of a decentralized snowball rolling downhill.' We were baffled but impressed.
*New Yorker*; June 8, 1940

June 28, 1940
## REPUBLICANS NOMINATE WENDELL WILLKIE FOR PRESIDENT

I have never even heard my son speak of a third term.
Sara Roosevelt; 1939

July 18, 1940
## ROOSEVELT RENOMINATED ON 1ST BALLOT

Like most men of my age, I had made plans for myself, plans for a private life of my own choice and for my own satisfaction, a life of that kind to begin in January, 1941. These plans, like so many other plans, had been made in a world which now seems as distant as another planet. Today all private plans, all private lives have been in a sense repealed by an over-riding public danger. In the face of that public danger all those who can be of service to the republic have no choice but to offer themselves for service in those capacities for which they may be fitted.

These, my friends, are the reasons why I have had to admit to myself, and now to state to you, that my conscience will not let me turn back upon a call to service.
Franklin D. Roosevelt; nomination acceptance; July, 1940

Call him the gentleman from Indiana. Call him the candidate of the Republican party. Call him our opponent. Call him anything, but never call him bad names. That creates an unfavorable impression among Americans. And never mention his name. Many people, hundreds of people, cannot remember names. If they don't hear the opponent's name that is clear gain for us. They have heard my name so often and so long that it in itself is a political asset, and you can trust them, particularly the Roosevelt-haters, to say my name plenty of times. In the end, lots of people go to the polls and look the list of candidates over and make up their minds after they get into the ballot booth. I know that may sound feeble-minded, but I know it's true. When they look over the list they vote for people whose names they know. We don't want to do anything to advertise the name of the opposing candidate.
Franklin D. Roosevelt to campaign aide; 1940

I cannot follow the President in his conduct of foreign affairs in this critical time. There have been occasions when many of us have wondered if he was not deliberately inciting us to war . . . He has secretly meddled in the affairs of Europe, and he has even unscrupulously urged other countries to hope for more help than we are able to give . . . But while he has been quick to thus tell other nations what they ought to do, Mr. Roosevelt has been slow to take the American people into his confidence.

If I am elected President . . . I plan to reverse both these policies. I should threaten foreign governments only when our country was threatened by them and when I was ready to act; and I should consider our diplomacy as part of the people's business.
Wendell Willkie; nomination acceptance; August, 1940

I have a great stake in this country. My wife and I have given nine hostages to fortune.

Our children and your children are more important than anything else in the world. The kind of America that they and their children will inherit is of grave concern to us all. In the light of these considerations, I believe that Franklin D. Roosevelt should be re-elected President of the United States.
Joseph P. Kennedy; 1940

**Joseph P. Kennedy with sons—left, John F. and right, Joe, Jr.**

Opposite above: Father Charles Coughlin. Opposite below: FDR, inauguration day, 1941

If Mr. Roosevelt is re-elected . . . we will be buying gas masks for Christmas presents.
Father Charles Coughlin; *Social Justice*; July, 1940

It is as clear as anything on this earth that the United States will not go to war, *but* it is equally clear that war is coming, coming toward the Americas . . .
   Why are we sleeping, Americans? When are we going to wake up? When are we going to tell our government that we want to defend our homes and our children and our liberties whatever the cost in money or blood?
   Do we want to see Hitler in Independence Square? In Independence Hall? Making fun of the Liberty Bell? NO!
William C. Bullitt, Ambassador to France; 1940

September 4, 1940
**ROOSEVELT TRADES DESTROYERS FOR SEA BASES; TELLS CONGRESS HE ACTED ON OWN AUTHORITY**

September 7, 1940
**WILLKIE CONDEMNS DESTROYER TRADE; CALLS IT THE 'MOST ARBITRARY & DICTATORIAL ACTION EVER TAKEN BY A PRESIDENT"**

September 8, 1940
**LONDON ABLAZE UNDER WORST BOMBING OF WAR**

October 16, 1940
**16,000,000 TO ENROLL TODAY IN FIRST PEACETIME DRAFT; ALL IN THE U.S. BETWEEN 21 & 36, INCLUDING ALIENS, MUST HEED CALL**

October 30, 1940
**FIRST DRAFT NUMBER IS 158; PRESIDENT LEADS CEREMONY STARTING BIG CITIZEN ARMY**

Reicka Mary Schwancke, Austin [Texas] girl who registered for the draft was the 10th person in the city to have her serial number drawn in the draft lottery today.
   Roy T. Anderson, draft board chairman, has been instructed to classify her 4F, for persons 'physically unfit for service.'
*New York Times*; October 31, 1940

To the sixteen million young men who register today, I say that democracy is your cause—the cause of youth.
Franklin D. Roosevelt; October 16, 1940

Vote for Willkie to avert war and stop dictatorship.
*Social Justice*; November, 1940

We are not old enough to have an indispensable man . . . We don't have to have a third term.
Wendell Willkie; 1940

November 7, 1940
## ROOSEVELT RE-ELECTED; VOTE ENDORSES FDR WAR STAND

Just hand me my old Martin, for soon I will be startin'
Back to dear old Charleston far away;
Since Roosevelt's been re-elected, we'll not be neglected,
We've got Franklin D. Roosevelt back again.

Back again, back again, back again, back again,
We've got Franklin D. Roosevelt back again;
Since Roosevelt's been elected, moonshine liquor's been corrected,
We've got legal wine, whiskey, beer and gin.

I'll take a drink of brandy and let myself be handy,
Good times are coming back again;
You can laugh and tell a joke, you can dance and drink and smoke,
We've got Franklin D. Roosevelt back again.

Back again, back again, back again, back again,
We've got Franklin D. Roosevelt back again;
We'll all have money in our jeans, we can travel with the queen,
We've got Franklin D. Roosevelt back again.

No more breadlines we're glad to say, the donkey won election day,
No more standing in the blowing snowing rain;
He's got things in full sway, we're all working and getting our pay,
We've got Franklin D. Roosevelt back again.
**We've Got Franklin D. Roosevelt Back Again**; song; Cohen and Seeger; 1940

One thing that is necessary for American national defense is additional productive facilities; and the more we increase those facilities—factories, shipbuilding ways, munitions plants, et cetera and so on—the stronger American national defense is. Now, orders from Great Britain are therefore a tremendous asset to American national defense, because they create, automatically, additional facilities. I am talking selfishly, from the American point of view—nothing else.
Franklin D. Roosevelt; December 17, 1940

January 7, 1941
## ROOSEVELT ASKS ALL-OUT AID TO DEMOCRACIES; TO SEND THEM SHIPS, PLANES, TANKS AND GUNS; DENIES ACT OF WAR

January 11, 1941
## BILL GIVES PRESIDENT UNLIMITED POWER TO LEND WAR EQUIPMENT & RESOURCES; GOES TO CONGRESS; QUICK ACTION URGED

Suppose my neighbor's home catches fire, and I have got a length of garden hose four or five hundred feet away; but, by Heaven, if he can take my garden hose and connect it up with his hydrant, I may help him to put out his fire. Now, what do I do? I don't say to him before that operation, 'Neighbor, my garden hose cost me $15; you have got to pay me $15 for it.' What is the transaction that goes on? I don't want $15—I want my garden hose back after the fire is over. All right. If it goes through the fire all right, intact, without any damage to it, he gives it back to me and thanks me very much for the use of it. But suppose it gets smashed up—holes in it—during the fire; we don't have to have too much formality about it, but I can say to him, 'I was glad to lend you that hose; I see I can't use it any more, it's all smashed up.' He says, 'How many feet of it were there?' I tell him, 'There were 150 feet of it.' He says, 'All right, I will replace it.' Now, if I get a nice garden hose back, I am in pretty good shape. In other words, if you lend certain munitions and get the munitions back at the end of the war, if they are intact—haven't been hurt—you are all right; if they have been damaged or deteriorated or lost completely, it seems to me that you come out pretty well if you have them replaced by the fellow that you have lent them to.
Franklin D. Roosevelt; December 17, 1940

January 24, 1941
## LINDBERGH SEES STALEMATE; 'MISTAKE' TO AID BRITAIN; 'THIS PROLONGS WAR' HE SAYS

The recent House bill 1776, called the Lend-Lease Bill, seeks to confer upon the President authority unheard of in our history. It seeks to vest in the Executive powers which the President says he does not want and would not accept but for the emergency. The opponents of the Bill claim that it amounts to an abdication by Congress of its responsibility and that it is not necessary at this time.

Personally, I am a great believer in centralized responsibility and therefore believe in conferring all powers necessary to carry out that responsibility. Moreover, I appreciate full well that time is of the essence.

Nevertheless, I am unable to agree with the proponents of this bill that it has yet been shown that we face such immediate danger as to justify this surrender of the authority and responsibility of the Congress.
Joseph P. Kennedy; February, 1941

The Lend-Lease bill is not substantially concerned with lending or leasing or giving materials to Britain. It is concerned, however, with the scuttling of the last vestige of democracy in the world—American democracy . . .
    The Lend-Lease bill will substitute Karl Marx for George Washington.
Father Charles Coughlin; *Social Justice*; February 3, 1941

March 9, 1941
## SENATE PASSES AID-TO-BRITAIN BILL 60-31; ALL CURBS DOWNED

This decision is the end of any attempts at appeasement in our land; the end of urging us to get along with dictators; the end of compromise with tyranny and the forces of oppression.
Franklin D. Roosevelt; March 15, 1941

August 11, 1941
## ROOSEVELT RETURNS TO WHITE HOUSE: REVEALS 'SECRET' MEETING AT SEA WITH BRITISH PRIME MINISTER

August 19, 1941
## SELECTIVE SERVICE ACT EXTENDED BY CONGRESS; PASSES BY ONE VOTE

This vote clearly indicates that the Administration could not get a resolution through the Congress for a declaration of war . . . It is also noticed that the Congress does not take seriously the cry of the Administration that the so-called emergency is greater now than it was a year ago.
Senator Burton K. Wheeler; August, 1941

Gentlemen, you all know how difficult my mission is. But I'll do all I can to make it a successful one for the sake of two countries, Japan and the United States.
Japanese Special Envoy Kurusu; November, 1941

**Japanese Special Envoy Kurusu**

157

The Honorable Franklin D. Roosevelt
President of the United States
Washington, D.C.

America First Committee,
New York Chapter, Inc.
December 6, 1941

Dear Mr. President:

What is all this sabre rattling in connection with Japan? Why are our sons wanted to fight a war 10,000 miles away—must we close our eyes to our urgent domestic problems—merely to guard and defend the capitalistic holdings of millionaire corporations of this country and ENGLAND?

Why are you so deeply aggrieved over the progress Japan has made on the continent of Asia? Of course, it seems obvious that if Japan does not conquer disunited China—some other force will—and it probably will be *Communism*. Is our Administration keenly concerned about checking Japan's progress—merely to assist Communizing China? It is a safe guess that if Japan did conquer China, occidental industrial moguls of the so-called 'democracies' would lose their grip on the natural resources which *God* has placed over there for the people of *that* part of the world.

Are our sons expected to fight to protect these holdings of the British and the large corporations of the United States—merely because their wealthy corporations want to get their raw material from places where they have to pay for them on the basis of a working man's wage of twenty-five to thirty cents a day—rather than pay their own citizens a decent wage for the same labor at home? Of course, no other great power (who might emulate our own methods of expansion) should be allowed to conquer China and consequently develop it as part of a great nation. No, no, this would be contrary to the plan of the British and American financial magnates whose particular desire seems to be to keep China *disunited*: disunited, so these financial powers may continue to *own* all that God has put there for *those* people to either use for themselves or to be compensated for —in foreign trade—on a fair and square basis.

This is the real reason you want our sons to fight for 'American interests' in the Far East. We emphatically reiterate that this is not enough reason to satisfy American mothers and fathers who are expected to sacrifice their sons.

You tell us that we must check Japan's aggression—that we must protect the Burma Road—that we must protect Siam.

We are keenly aware of this subterfuge.

In regard to Japan's aggression—10,000 miles away—let us not forget the expansion process of our own nation—let us not forget how we got Texas, California—don't overlook the Mexican War—and we American citizens are keenly aware of the aggressive hand our government has consistently played in Latin-American affairs. Has Japan anything to say about that?

Now, about the Burma Road—we sincerely believe our own Lincoln Highway could be better policed—and that our President should steer us off the 'Road to Financial Ruin'—before concerning ourselves with the Burma Road—thousands of miles away—in which we will not permit our sons to become involved.

We want to make it definitely understood that the reasons thus far advanced by the Administration for a 'show-down' with Japan are not nearly sufficient to send American soldiers abroad to fight!

Respectfully yours,
Leonard N. Conrad (signed)
Chairman

## PEARL HARBOR IS BOMBED BY JAP AIR FORCE; CONGRESS ANSWERS ATTACK TODAY; LIGHTNING CHANGE FROM ALL-OUT AID TO REAL WAR

Yesterday, December 7, 1941—a date which will live in infamy—the United States of America was suddenly and deliberately attacked by the Empire of Japan . . .

It will be recorded that the distance of Hawaii from Japan makes it obvious that the attack was deliberately planned many days or even weeks ago. During the intervening time the Japanese Government has deliberately sought to deceive the United States by false statements and expressions of hope for continued peace.

The attack yesterday on the Hawaiian Islands has caused severe damage to American naval and military forces. I regret to tell you that very many American lives have been lost . . .

No matter how long it may take us to overcome this premeditated invasion, the American people in their righteous might will win through to absolute victory . . .

I ask that Congress declare that since the unprovoked and dastardly attack by Japan on Sunday, December seventh, 1941, a state of war has existed between the United States and the Japanese Empire.

Franklin D. Roosevelt; December 8, 1941

The Honorable Franklin D. Roosevelt
President of the United States
Washington, D.C.

America First Committee,
New York Chapter, Inc.
December 8, 1941

Dear Mr. President:

In view of the fact that we are now at war with Japan, please consider the contents of our letter, dated December 6, 1941, null and void.

We stand behind you in your endeavor to win this war. We pledge you our support.

Respectfully yours,
Leonard N. Conrad (signed)
Chairman

# Index

# Acknowledgments

## Picture Credits

**Associated Press-Wide World** 52, 63, 82, 148, 155 top

**Bettmann Archive** 22, 50, 60, 79 right, 80

**Culver Pictures** 12, 54, 146–147

**Detroit News** 14

**Federal Bureau of Investigation** 78

**Franklin D. Roosevelt Library** 2–3 (RA-Rothstein), 18, 148, 62, 84–85, 88 (FSA-Shahn), 93 (FSA-Rothstein), 98 bottom (FSA-Shahn), 102 center, 102–103 top (WPA), 104–105 (NAACP), 116 top & center, 150 top, 151, 154 left

**John E. Allen** 64–65, 67, 122, 124–125 bottom, 126, 128, 131 left & right, 132, 133 top & bottom, 137, 138, 139 right, 141

**Library of Congress** 6–7, 20 (FSA-Lange), 58 (FSA-Delano), 66, 85 (FSA-Lange), 94 top (FSA-Mydans), 94 bottom, 98 top (FSA-Shahn), 99 (RA-Shahn), 115, 117 bottom, 129, 146 bottom left, 154 (FSA-Brown)

**Museum of the City of New York** 24, 138 left, rear endpapers (all Berenice Abbott)

**Museum of Modern Art** 123

**National Archives** (US Information Agency unless otherwise indicated) 19, 51, 53, 56, 59 (WPA), 60–61 (CCC), 61, 69, 72, 75, 97 (WPA), 102 bottom (WPA), 103 (WPA), 110, 112 (WPA), 120–121 bottom, 136, 140

**National Archives-Motion Picture Division** (Universal News unless otherwise indicated) 1, 41, 43, 76 (FBI), 77 (FBI), 86, 124–125 top, 146 top (Signal Corps), 147 top (Signal Corps), 157, 158–159 (Signal Corps)

**New York Daily News** 38

**New York Public Library**: front endpapers (FSA-Lange), 9, 24 inset, 49, 79 (FSA), 91 (FSA-Shahn), 92, 100, 101, 116 bottom (FSA-Lange), 130 (FSA-Vachon), 134–135, 150

**Oakland Museum** 17 (Lange)

**Underwood & Underwood** 8, 30 bottom, 31

**United Press International-Acme** 10, 25, 26–27, 28, 29, 30 top, 32, 33, 34–35, 36, 40, 44–45, 46–47, 57, 60, 108, 117 top, 118, 120–121 top, 121 top, 142–143, 144, 148 top, 150 inset, 152–153, 153, 155 bottom, 156

## Literary acknowledgments

The publishers wish to thank the following for permission to reprint quoted extracts:

Federal Bureau of Investigation and Little, Brown & Co., for **Persons in Hiding** by J. Edgar Hoover; © 1938, 1968 by J. Edgar Hoover; used by permission (pp. 68, 78)

Harcourt, Brace, Jovanovich, Inc., for **The Daring Young Man on the Flying Trapeze** from *After Thirty Years: The Daring Young Man on the Flying Trapeze*; copyright © 1934, 1962 by William Saroyan; abridged and reprinted by permission (pp. 15–16)

Harold Ober Associates and Charles Scribner's Sons, for **On the Trail of Pat Hobby** by F. Scott Fitzgerald; copyright 1941 by Esquire, Inc., copyright renewed 1968 by Frances Scott Fitzgerald Smith. Reprinted by permission (pp. 132–134)

Harper's Magazine, for **The Collapse of Politics** by Elmer Davis; © 1932, 1959 by Harper's Magazine (pp. 48, 49–50)

Helga Green, for **Noon Street Nemesis**, from *The Smell of Fear* by Raymond Chandler; Hamish Hamilton, London; © 1965 by Helga Green; used by permission (pp. 67–68)

I.H.T. Corporation, for articles from *The New York Herald Tribune*: © copyright 1929 (pp. 10, 11); © 1932 (p. 72); © 1933 (pp. 61, 76); © 1934 (pp. 73–74, 78–83, 83) by the I.H.T. Corporation. Reprinted by permission.

Ladies Home Journal, for **A Story of Two Mustaches** by Henry Pringle; © 1940 by Downe Publishing, Inc. Reprinted with permission (pp. 138–139)

Leo Feist, Inc., for **Over the Rainbow**; lyrics by E. Y. Harburg, music by Harold Arlen; © 1939 by Leo Feist, Inc. Used with permission; all rights reserved (p. 103)

Little, Brown & Co., for **Invasion From Mars** from *The Panic Broadcast* by Howard Koch; © 1967 by Little, Brown & Co.; used by permission (p. 144)

Ludlow Music, Inc., for **Dust Can't Kill Me** by Woody Guthrie © 1963 (p. 98) and **End O' My Line** by Woody Guthrie © 1960 (p. 88); both copyrights by Ludlow Music, Inc. and distributed through TRO Essex Music, Ltd. All rights reserved, used by permission.

McIntosh and Otis and Viking Press, for **The Grapes of Wrath** by John Steinbeck © copyright 1939. Reprinted by permission (pp. 92, 95, 96)

New York Times Company, for articles from *The New York Times*: © copyright 1931 (pp. 70, 71); © 1932 (pp. 29, 36); © 1935 (pp. 78, 111, 113); © 1936 (p. 136); © 1937 (pp. 100, 102, 120); © 1939 (pp. 136, 149); © 1940 (pp. 139, 154); © 1941 (p. 141) by The New York Times Company. Reprinted by permission.

Readers Digest Association, Inc. for **Letters from the Dust Bowl** by Caroline Henderson © 1936 (pp. 89–90); **Unto Dust** by George Greenfield © 1937 (p. 90); **After the Deluge** by Thomas Kramer © 1937 (p. 102)

Saturday Evening Post, for **Star Spangled Fascists** by Stanley High © 1939 by The Curtis Publishing Co. Reprinted by permission (pp. 147–148)

Stormking Music, for **I Am a Union Woman** by Aunt Molly Jackson © 1966 by Stormking Music and distributed through Harmony Music, Ltd. All rights reserved, used by permission (p. 119)

Warner Bros., for the following songs: **Brother, Can You Spare a Dime?** by Jay Gorney and E. Y. Harburg © 1932 by Harms, Inc. (p. 34); **Happy Days Are Here Again** by Milton Ager and Jack Yellen © 1929 (p. 51); **Hooray for Hoolywood** by Johnny Mercer and Richard A. Whiting © 1937 (p. 129); **We're in the Money** by Harry Warren and Al Dubin © 1933 (p. 55). All copyrights renewed by Warner Bros. All rights reserved. Used by permission.

Will Rogers Memorial Commission of Claremore, Oklahoma, for all Will Rogers quotations. Used by permission (pp. 21, 53, 55, 58, 82)